MW01200051

Step away from the War

Tom Milton Peters

Step away from the War

Copyright © 2017 Tom Milton Peters

All rights reserved.

ISBN: 0692909885
ISBN-13: 978-0692909881

DEDICATION

Pat - waiting for my return home
Mitra - suggesting my return to VN
JoAn - loving encouragement

Step away from the War

CONTENTS

Step away from the War

ACKNOWLEDGMENTS

Thanks to my editor **Eric Mrozek**, at Free Eagle Studios. To **Lisette Rabinow-Palley, Lantz Simpson, Crystal Lagunas and Wendy O'Dea** for advice after reading a first draft. To **Lynne Fuqua** for pointing out the typos.
To **JoAn**, my wife, for the ever-present love, space and understanding.
A special thanks to a dear friend, **Mitra Moassessi** who suggested I go back to Vietnam.
And thank you, **John Plunkett**, for your friendship in that weird year and hanging in there with me throughout all these years since.

Step away from the War

PREFACE

It was an easy decision for me to write these memoirs. The reason...being told by dear friends and family members that I should tell my story. These moments come to mind.

- Seated in Dave's living room where Linda and Dave Peters first lived on London Street, listening to Jethro Tull in a state of bliss, circa 1972.

- Or on a boat anchored off some lake in Michigan with my brother, Bob, in one of our countless talks about life and love.

- I'm sure it was in my cousin's apartment across from the park looking out on the Detroit River, at the foot of Southfield. Dan Peters and I have shared many connected stories and memories of our grandfather, Raymond J. Peters. Dan and his sisters, Jane and Susan, lost their father, Raymond Peters, when they were young...my bond with these cousins is difficult to put into words. Ray was my father's older brother, an amazing presence to me, speaking his mind with my grandfather and father on subjects worth listening to.

- It happened in a eucalyptus scented backyard in California with Tom Walsh and his wife Barb with whom I lived with during many vacations. We may have touched the subject. Or were we at Tom Comb's place in Laguna Beach?

- Lying on lounge chairs on the patio of a majestic home in Prescott, Arizona, waiting for a shooting star, after a wonderful meal, drinking fine wine and chilled martinis. Christine Abbate, wife to Gary, suggested writing it down.

- Sitting in Houston's in Scottsdale, Arizona, with Karen and Horace Allen and I swear the subject of writing shit down came up. Our chats were long and intoxicating. Just can't get over how delicious their martinis taste and how they refresh their cold goodness with a new martini glass from the freezer half way through the drinking experience.

- Maybe it was playing golf with Lantz Simpson when sharing stories bigger than golf itself.

- Seated at a large table in a

secluded area of the Grange Restaurant at the Citizens Hotel in Sacramento with my dear friend and former president of our faculty union, Mitra Moassessi, Pete Morse, our current president and a Polo Lounge pal, Kevin Menton, Matt Hotsinpiller, Kym McBride, Dennis Frisch, Fran Chandler, Cathy Matheson, Jackie Scott, Elaine Rogue, George Davison, Tom Chen, Mario Martinez, Tracy Ellie, Craig Mohr, Howard Stahl...

- WAIT maybe it was the hole in the wall, local bar Matt and Kevin found ourselves in ...after the aforementioned gathering. We met a higher being in coke bottle glasses and a strong presence... under a lot of influence. Anyway, I'm sure the idea of a memoir came up but maybe it was directed to the higher being.

When I set out writing, it was only going to be my one weird year in Vietnam.

Broadening the scope to fill in remaining years is what I present to you in 12 chapters.

As my daughter, Ellie, would say, "Don't judge me."

V

Step away from the War

CHAPTER 1

PRELUDE TO THE YEAR OF WAR

The turning point in my life was when I turned 20 years old. Up until that time, I was drifting along, care-free and irresponsible, doing things my way and fucking up, frequently.

At six years old, my parents must have thought I was responsible. I was put in charge of walking my younger brother, Dave, to his first day of kindergarten at Foote Elementary School.

"In case you get out early, just walk out the school door, turn left, show me your left, good, then walk the short two blocks to London Street, you'll recognize that, then make one more left and our house is three doors down on the right. 1724, got it?" I instructed Dave.

"Got it," he said.

After school, no Dave anywhere.

I assumed that he would walk out of the front door of the school. It was only when I found him near Fort Street that I realize my mistake. He walked out a side door and made a left turn, and just kept walking.

After that incident, I was demoted to changing the diapers of our newborn twin sisters, Janet and Joan. In a little over two years, Joyce and Sharon would arrive. About four years of helping my mother change countless cotton diapers and soaking them in a white pail with a strong mixture of water and ammonia, instilled some sense of responsibility.

In my very young eyes, the matriarch of the family was my mother. However, for a brief period, I felt the patriarch of the family was my paternal grandfather.

My grandfather was the city clerk of River Rouge, Michigan for more than 20 years. His three-story house had a rock garden in the back, a scary coal bin in the basement, a Florida room in the back of the house with an impressive desk, and footbath near the back door by the kitchen. I can almost smell the rich wood oak banister that led to upstairs bedrooms and a mysterious third floor attic. A piano and a fireplace adorned the living room, doilies lay on tables and arms of chairs and couches, and a big porch that had a swinging bench. The time I spent in this house had a smell of hope.

The sense of peace I experienced at my grandparent's home was juxtaposed to the chaotic life in our little two-story townhome at 254½ Goodell Street, directly adjacent to a portion of the steel mill. Upon revisiting as an adult, I noticed it was more like cheap projects, than townhomes.

Shortly after I turned five, I began to bond with my father. Before that time, I felt a certain 'strength and presence' in my grandfather and Uncle Ray, I didn't feel in my father. I may have thought my grandfather was the smartest man of the family, and my uncle the strongest, but soon figured out, my father was the most resourceful and hard-working. This change occurred while having the family house built on London Street in Lincoln Park, Michigan.

When the family got into the old Plymouth and drove to the worksite, it was little more than three empty cement

4

basements. Three almost identical two bedroom bungalows with functional attics were going to be built with chain-link fences around each backyard. To my delight, the three acres behind the new houses was dense woods that would become my play area for the next five years.

As the skeleton of the house went up, my brother, Dave, and I were allowed to run about and witness how the house was being constructed. Once, I talked him down a plank into a newly poured basement, then lifted the plank. He screamed so I got quite the spanking.

The frame of the house would be built and I would listen as my father would explain to my mother in detail why this and that thickness of wood would be used to frame a door or window. He had a keen knowledge of how practical things were put together and how they worked.

My mother was scheduled to have twins and my father planned to finish off the attic after the house was built. It was for our baby brother Gary, Dave and I to share as a bedroom. To this day, the smell of fresh pine wood reminds me of helping my father finish out that attic. I learned the precision of the work he would perform and the swear words used when things didn't go quite the way he intended.

My father would work eight hours at the mill, then come home and work on that attic for a few hours, then he worked most of the weekends. Whenever the car broke down, my father would fix it. Once when the washing machine broke down, he completely de-assembled it in the basement, spreading each piece in the exact order it was taken apart, replace a $2 gasket and put it all back together, and it worked.

"If something was made by a human, then a human like me can fix it if it breaks." He once said to me.

That statement stuck with me. This work ethic gave me respect for my father.

Though I hung onto respect for my father over the years, it was difficult to like him. The only physical contact I experienced with him was violent. When I screwed up, out came the leather belt and I was whipped with it on my behind. If the belt wasn't close, it was with his hand. The 'whippin' had to be hard enough to make me scream and cry and my younger brothers had to watch as a lesson. They occasionally didn't get the lesson straight and received their own whippin. This was hard to watch.

Being raised in the mid-1950s, I don't think I ever witnessed a father hugging a young son except on a TV show like "Lassie". I think I wished for that hug. It never came. That's just how some fathers were back then, and I'll guess they learned this behavior from their fathers.

At 10 years old, I became as monetarily independent as I could with a newspaper route, delivering the *Detroit Free Press* in the wee hours of the morning to about 80 customers on my bicycle. Occasionally, stopping at the local White Castle for six tiny, greasy burgers, a breakfast treat when famished.

I remember buying my mother a cheap, chaise lounge chair for no reason other than I knew she got tired during the day. Looking back with 20/20 hindsight, that gesture may have been the beginning of competition between my father and I, to please my mother. That contest intensified over the years after I returned from Vietnam. I imagine my father hearing, Tom this and Tom that, way too many times. I was forceful about eliminating the 'N' word from our family's vocabulary. Once got in my father's face about smacking my brother Bob.

In the last few years of his life, my father had the habit of pronouncing my name Thom-ass. I couldn't imagine what was going through his mind. I had forced him to hug me and say the 'L' word, but he probably sensed my unease with him.

Even in the 1990s, family or personal therapy was taboo in working class families like ours as far as I could see, but we sure could have benefited from it. Life is complicated, some things you just let pass and move on.

In the summer before I entered seventh grade, I met a young man whose family had just moved north from Kentucky into the trailer park on the other side of the woods from our house. Richard Peel was my age, with a small, but athletic build. He played baseball with us in the field near Dix highway behind the Fly-In Bar with passion. We played baseball from after breakfast until the street lights came on in the evening, only stopping to eat lunch.

Richard didn't show up for a couple of days, someone who knew the trailer he lived in, went to find out if he was OK. A neighbor of Richard's informed us that he had come home from playing ball with us a couple of days earlier with a headache, and then died that next morning from an aneurysm in his brain.

My disbelieve warped into an obsessive thought. He was with us, playing baseball with agility and gusto...then he just...dies!

No funeral, just an awkward moment some days later at Huff Junior High School when our 7th grade homeroom teacher calls out Richard's name just before mine and I, casually hiding my pain, let the teacher know...he died.

Three months later President John F. Kennedy was assassinated, shocking the nation and leaving a generation with less hope for the future. I was still obsessed with Richard Peel's death, now we all sat glued to the black & white TV, watching all the bloody details and the heart-breaking funeral of our president.

The freedom of my younger days, filled me with the wonder of nature and the building of social skills I've enjoyed all my life. But as I moved into my teens, a nagging inclination to please everyone and attract some attention would work against me.

Naturally, girls became a big deal, we all flocked to what was called 'the quarry' to hang out in the sun. Slick tanned, youthful bodies smeared with baby oil, the Rolling Stones playing in the background. "I Can't Get No Satisfaction" was a huge hit at the time, sort of a theme song for a generation aware that it may not find what it's looking for.

Since the quarry was 12 miles south of Lincoln Park, you had to have access to a car to get there. If an older friend wasn't around to drive, I would convince a friend to steal a car from the used-car lots on Fort St. We took Chevys because if the key holder was left in the 'On' position instead of 'Lock', you didn't need a key to start the car.

One day I drove a blue Chevy station wagon back from the quarry. My friend noticed a police car behind us so I turned right at the next corner. The police notice my speed and pursued us. Our fathers were called to the police station to give us a couple of good smacks to the side of the head. After that the police let us go. The entire experience taught me that I shouldn't get caught.

The three years I spent in Lincoln Park High School were full of friends, fun, plenty of beer, and mediocre grades. I had a girlfriend named Nancy and a 1954 stick shift Chevy that I paid $50 for, and thanks to a friend, Jim Dotson, for letting me make payments of $10 a week from my job at Krupa's Supermarket. I immediately spray-painted a number 13 on both sides. At the time, few people knew that the number was a coded M for marijuana. I didn't even try the drug until I arrived in South Vietnam.

My other friends owned cheap cars, so we played this crazy game in the parking lot behind the Lincoln Park Plaza. We rolled down the windows and had somebody on the passenger side ram an opponent's car with a shopping cart.

The Chevy burned a quart of oil a day and I had to go to the Purple Martin gas station next to the plaza to buy recycled oil at 15 cents a quart. My father would borrow my car one day and get a ticket for excessive smoke.

In the Lincoln Park Plaza was a pizzeria name Colarossi's where we used to hang out quite a bit and invented the fine art of getting melted cheese balls from the pizzas to stick to the ceiling or the large white globe lights.

One other popular hangout was the McDonald's on Dix Highway, where we might stick a few friends in the trunk of our car and sneak them into the local drive in movie. It was also a hang out to find out where the weekend parties were taking place. Beer was a big deal, we always had to find characters around 21 years old to buy beer for us. We would congregate at Bruce Martinson's house often because his older brother would 'buy' for us. I couldn't hold my beer, and occasionally, I was caught pouring some out to try, in some way, to keep my shit together. But, drinking too much and throwing up was all part of the scene then, as was placing cherry bombs in phone booths, racing cars on deserted stretch of roads, driving to Toledo where the drinking age was 18 and bringing fake ID, and going to dances at the bandshell on Fort Street where popular bands had cool hair-dos.

When 1967 rolled around, I was a credit short of what I needed to graduate high school, so I had to take a summer class. Later, I went to work at Great Lakes Steel.

In 1968, I met my future wife, Patricia, and eloped with her in October when it became apparent I was going to be drafted. The draft notice instructed me to report to Fort Wayne, a Civil War era fort, near downtown Detroit in late December.

I had a scare at the induction center when we were told to line up single file and count off by fours. When the Drill Sergeant asked all the number twos to step forward, he welcomed these poor souls to the US Marine Corps. Fortunately, I was a number 3!

A few days after New Year's Day, 1969, I found myself on a bus headed to basic training at Fort Knox, Kentucky. Our fingers froze on the rifle range in the extreme cold of that winter. Getting up so early in the morning while still dark to put on all our gear and run a hilly mile before breakfast got us in shape. Returning to the mess hall to the smell of bacon and an appetite I had never experienced before was a memory that stuck with me. The competitive spirit in me, coupled with my fascination of never having fired a weapon before, resulted in me getting expert rating on the M14 rifle and the M60 machine gun. I look back in disbelieve that I wouldn't put it together that by scoring so well with these weapons, I'd find myself on a fast track to Advance Infantry Training at Fort Polk, Louisiana.

The bus ride to Louisiana took us through miles and miles of swamp and dead trees, giving me the overwhelming sensation of the misery to come.

Fort Polk sat on dusty, red clay and was hot. Hot like I had never experienced before then. The huge pine trees trapped the hot air and blocked any chance of a breeze. This was excellent training grounds for future Vietnam soldiers.

Sadly, two soldiers died in barracks near us from spinal meningitis, we were all quarantined to the fort without leave for six weeks.

As you may well imagine, I got my orders to take a 30 day leave at the end of April 1969, to report to Fort Lewis, Washington. Two days processing papers, collecting combat apparel for overseas duty to South Vietnam. The flight landed me in Anchorage, Alaska; Tokyo, Japan and finally, Cam Ranh Bay, South Vietnam.

On my last morning before embarking on this yearlong odyssey, my father was in his car ready to leave for work with sunglasses on. We exchanged goodbyes through the open window, he may have said 'be careful'. I always felt I could have used a hug. The sunglasses were dark, I thought, maybe he had a tear in his eye.

CHAPTER 2

FIRST ENCOUNTER

*Out beyond ideas of wrongdoing and
rightdoing, there is a field.*

I'll meet you there.

Rumi

I met a lot of young men that day. I
don't exactly remember meeting Dene.
He was a tall, light-skinned African-
American who spoke Spanish fluently and
called me *amigo* from the very beginning
of our friendship. He had been in-country
a few months already and had seen too
much action; I could see it in his eyes.
Eyes that appeared resigned to accept
the inevitable. A violent death, in the

19

thick, muggy fields of South Vietnam.

We gathered at our unit's firebase just west of Tay Ninh. We were ordered to be ready to go out on a mission the next day. Was it Tuesday, Wednesday or Friday? What day of the week mattered no more. After two-weeks of training at our arrival point Cam Ranh Bay, I still felt ill prepared for what was to come.

I slept very little the night before. Thoughts of the recent past few weeks since arriving, plus every newsreel and TV news footage on Vietnam, filled my mind until dawn.

When we geared up that morning, I felt sick to my stomach. The whole platoon gathered in the wet, pre-dawn air, waiting for the lieutenant to give us the order to move to the chopper pad. Five of us were brand new to the platoon and didn't have a clue of what to do. I understood it was going to be an ugly, hot, miserable experience. Unfortunately, I still had 347 days left in my tour in-country. This was a countdown shared with thousands of other drafted soldiers.

Our main mode of transportation was the Bell UH-1D Huey. Flying on these workhorses was an experience I would have throughout my tour of duty.

On that first morning, Dene looked perplexed at all the activity.

"This seems unusual because the whole company is going on this mission and it would take a large flock of choppers to do the maneuver." He said.

As the Hueys landed, we were told to hurry into the open-aired, door-less cabins, as fast as we could.

When I got into a chopper, I could tell the experienced grunts from the newbies. The experienced infantrymen carelessly dangled their legs over the edge, whereas the newbies nestled in as close to the core of the chopper as possible.

The chopper raced above the rice paddies traveling at nearly 200 knots per hour. It was 'holy shit' fast. It didn't seem like we were in air that long before the choppers landed. After putting our feet on the ground, we all scurried over to a designated wood line and awaited further instructions.

Apparently the day before, Bravo company had engaged a North Vietnamese Army (NVA) force that was only a click or two away. We were told that they were a possibly battalion of well dug in regulars. I tried to get a clue of how much danger we were in from Dene. He tried his best to make sure we didn't feel too scared or overwhelmed. If Dene was going to live another day, we felt that we had a chance.

We were told to stay put inside the wood line, while the officers radioed in air support. The smell of the damp vegetation reminded me of the woods behind my childhood home, but these thoughts were quickly erased as the first two fighter jets made their low approach. I looked up in time to see the jet closest to us drop a tumbling bomb and its impact shook the ground violently.

Five minutes later, a single jet reappeared and dropped a second bomb, creating the same ground-shaking explosion. The other jet followed about a half minute later. It dropped its deadly load so close to us that giant pieces of shrapnel struck the trees above us. Luckily, the entire unit lay close to the ground and stayed there.

When the jets disappeared and we were told to wait. The area where the enemy was dug in was going to be bombarded by artillery shells. We commented that the air attack had to have killed every NVA soldier and living organism in those woods.

"You'd be surprised what the dug-in enemy can withstand." Dene smiled.

Listening to the lieutenant radio in the artillery attack was fascinating. I caught myself wishing that the lieutenant was my father and that Dene was my older brother coming up with a plan to save all my neighborhood pals from some unseen horror. The first round that comes in from the firebase was a puff of white smoke fifty feet above our position. The marker rounds gave the lieutenant a way to visually correct the artillery crew. Dene got a funny look on his face.

"He'll do some adjusting," he said.

The second puff of smoke appeared over our landing zone so the lieutenant called in a third correction. When another puff of smoke appeared at the dark wood line he chatters some orders on the radio and turned to us a bit surprised at our intense attention. A few minutes later, shells started dropping on the targeted area. The barrage went on for the next half hour. The air was filled with smoke, the smell of gunpowder and unimaginable sounds which forced us to lay low and cover our ears.

When the artillery attack was over, we moved across the open area between the wood lines and towards the enemy. There was a creepy quiet as we entered the wood line which gave us a false sense of security. I took point but I felt a sense of comfort because Dene was directly behind me. He directed me to walk slowly and be on the ready.

We were a few hundred feet inside the thick forest when the shots rang out and we all hit the ground. The combined scent of gunpowder and damp ground pressed against my face evolved into a future love of truffle mushrooms and a dislike for 4th of July fireworks. I naturally expected to be quite traumatized, but I was distracted by the fact that I had dropped down onto an army of red ants.

Okay, let me get this straight, I thought. *I'm getting my first dose of being shot at AND being bitten repeatedly by vicious red ants.*

The deafening noise of gunfire and explosions drowned out my screams.

"Are you hit?" Dene yelled.

"These ants are eating me alive," I shouted.

As the battle raged, I was stuck in time with burning agony. A few moments later, Dene grabbed my ankles and dragged me back toward the edge of the wood line. I was hauled to my feet, turned in the correct direction and told to run. Dene, several other grunts, and me bolted across the field to the wooded area where we originally assembled. Once we were somewhat safe, I ripped off my gear and fatigues to root out the red ants. Dene helped, but I didn't realize how much he had done until an hour had passed.

"It's alright amigo, he said. "We'll get out of this. We'll be fine. You'll see. Watch what happens next."

So, we all sat scared shitless for the rest of the morning and into the afternoon as Cobra gunships, fighter jets and artillery pounded the area where the NVA were dug in. We were witnessing a spectacle.

I'm sure glad the enemy doesn't have this kind of firepower. I thought.

"You saved my life back there", I

said to Dene.

"Bullshit, amigo," Dene replied. "We need a point man and you're it."

"Thanks, I think"

We laughed.

Every new man in the platoon tried to focus on a combat veteran. When we trained for deployment and instilled with the idea that the pecking order of respect depended upon combat experience. The other new grunts watched every move that combat vets were making, but I was talking to one. It gave me a real sense of comfort when I thought I'd be too scared and nervous to do anything.

The lieutenant kept himself busy all afternoon on the radio. The ground shook and the deafening bombs and minigun fire assaulted our ears.

In the late afternoon, we gobbled up

some C-rations and prepared for the next assault. We were told that we were going to be assisted by the South Vietnam (ARVN) marines. Dene kept assuring me that there wasn't going to be anyone left to assault.

We entered the dark wood line like we once had, some hours earlier, but the ARVN Marines had not arrived yet. Our platoon, flanked by two other platoons from C Company and one from B Company, all spread out over a wide area and moved cautiously. The slow walk was surreal because of the dense smell of gunpowder, occasional pungent stink of death, made so strong by the intense, stifling humidity.

About 100 paces inside, we took on small arms fire; we all hit the ground in disbelief. Hugging the ground as close as I could, I positioned myself behind a tree that seemed much too narrow. Dene yelled at us to stay put. The fire was sporadic but when the bursts came, we laid as low as possible. This firing went on for what seemed like forever when we heard the strange sound of a whistle behind us. Dene said, "The AVRN Marines are here." He laid only about 10 feet away from me and had a smile on his face. Next thing I know a Marine grunt is crouched next to me. Their Captain blew his whistle once and about 20 or 25 Marines charged forward.

"Look at those crazy mother fuckers, Amigo!"

The shooting was intense for a short ten minutes and the Marines overran the NVA bunkers, killing all occupants. War's stark and deadly reality hits me; I will never be the same after this day. Death doesn't merely lie in a coffin quietly; it hits you in the face.

We were able to advance a couple

of hundred feet when an RPG (rocket propelled grenade) killed one of the ARVNs. We returned fire, this time with greater intensity. The enemy fired back with equal force, the ARVN Marines pushed on and we followed.

Orders came from command to retreat. The hour and a half it took us to get in as far as we did, would take less than five minutes to scurry out. We ran out of this dark, otherworldly forest into the landing zone or LZ opening and across to the opposite wood line. We were told to pull 50% guard all night, one grunt sleeping for every grunt on guard duty. Exhaustion helped our rest, but the occasional artillery bombardment throughout the night made anything resembling sleep, impossible.

On my second day out in the field of combat, I couldn't help but think that my year was going to end in my death.

The artillery bombardment stopped in the middle of my third shift on guard duty. Moments later, our lieutenant received orders from command to move back in at sunrise. Part of B Company and most of A Company were positioned on the backside of the thick woods. Troops from the 1st Cavalry were on the flanks to ensure the enemy couldn't retreat in any direction from our attack. When the sun rose, we checked our ammo supplies, gathered at the edge of the open field and followed the ARVN Marines across the field once more.

We maneuver around numerous bomb craters and the bunkers that had been previously assaulted. I quietly hoped the bombs ended this adventure when shots rang out ahead of us. One of the marines was hit. A medic quickly crawled to his aid. In response, we poured fire in the direction of the small arms attack. To our left, shots ring out from an AK47.

We keep firing on the bunkers and spider holes when a grenade goes off. An ARVN positioned himself close enough to a spider hole to roll a grenade into it and stop the crossfire.

Orders came from our lieutenant to bring the 90mm rocket launcher forward. We keep our distance, because of its dangerous back blast. While aimed at the bunker, an experienced sergeant trained an M72 LAW, light anti-tank weapon on the other bunker. The bunkers are silenced with two loud explosions.

As the morning heated up, we advance forward into the bomb crater debris filled woods. After a while, fire erupts again. Only this time, the shots seemed to be coming from every direction so we all took cover. I landed in a small bomb crater near a tree and was quickly joined by a sergeant named Carlos Mendez.

"We're pulling out to make way for another air strike." The sergeant said.

We crawl on the damp ground for at least 50 yards before we broke into a run. Once we hit the adjacent wood line, I collapsed from exhaustion like all of the others in my unit.

The air strikes that came an hour later were dramatic. We were warned to take cover because the Air Force was about to drop 500 lb. bombs. Several of us gathered at the edge of the trees to watch the show.

The jets roared over the enemy position and dropped their payload. I lay flat as the ground jumps beneath me. Shrapnel whirled through the air. Behind me, I heard a strange thud and a groan. Sergeant Mendez took a baseball-size piece of shrapnel in the chest, which made him fall on a grunt behind him.

"Medic!" the covered grunt screamed.

The sergeant was pale, awestricken and bleeding heavily. The medic covered the wound and applied pressure as four of us dragged him onto the stretcher and hauled him into the woods. The lieutenant quickly called in a medivac chopper.

Moments later, a second jet flew overhead which forced us to hit the ground. The piercing sound of shrapnel penetrated the trees around us and smoky pieces dropped near me. The next four passes by the jets were napalm drops. The flames leaped from the woods, providing new smells that I would never forget.

The medivac chopper arrived in between the air strike and another artillery bombardment. Resupplies were dropped in alongside the medical help, so we loaded up on ammo and C rations. By

6 o'clock, the bombing stopped. We prepared for another assault without the support from the ARVN Marines.

Our allies had taken on quite a few wounded, so the entire unit was evacuated. We were on our own.

Most of us felt some relief when we reached one of the craters left from the 500-lb. bombs. The crater was fifty or sixty feet across and about ten feet deep. Everything around the crater was smashed in a distinctive pattern which made it difficult to maneuver the area.

The scorched vegetation had the strong smell of petroleum caused by the napalm. By the time of our advance, most of the smoldering had been squelched by the high humidity and some periodic light rain. We looked at the second crater. It seemed similar to the previous one, but the indescribable smell and some of the unnatural debris signaled it was probably a direct hit on a main part of the tunnel complex. Bodies were now being found, but we were ordered to press on into the woods.

We took on some small arms fire when we reached a small clearing which forced us to crawl back into the thick forest. I recognized the spider hole location as the second AK47 burst rang out, firing at a right angle to my position. I crawled along the wood line motioning to three grunts that they should not fire in my direction.

I didn't want anything to do with this friendly fire shit.

Once I got within tossing distance, I rolled a baseball grenade into the hole. An explosion sent a pith helmet high into the air, landing in the small open patch. I had silenced the spider hole. A new grunt named Rios grabbed the helmet souvenir and put it on over his Army-issued helmet with a grin. He soon discovered that part of the previous occupant's cranial remains were lodged inside.

We cleared the rest of the wooded area without further incidents. After another restless night, we were choppered back to the firebase.

That morning, I joined the daredevil, leg danglers on our flight back.

I lost my combat virginity in my first days in the field. Dene and I received Bronze Stars and joked about them, wishing we could trade them for an early return home.

Bravery was mentioned in our award citations, but we knew the unsung heroes of that mission were the ARVN Marines.

CHAPTER 3

STAYING ALIVE

*We just wanted to stay alive and
forget about the horrors of combat
from a cheap lawn chair, back home.*

There was an extreme richness to
the smell of the country, aided by the
dense heat and humidity, human waste
and sweat, animal dung and the sweet,
fuel scent of napalm.

Our side was literally dropping fire
on the enemy. Innocence evaporated
within me. I'm now an accomplice to these
human atrocities. I made a momentary
connection to my childhood past. The loss

of my sexual innocence discovered in a Playboy magazine in an old, abandoned truck in the alley near our home. That truck had a strong smell, similar to napalm.

The first encounter formed a tightly woven fabric of fear that shaped the remaining 347 days left in country. News from home of Neil Armstrong's first steps on the moon, Woodstock, student protests, and talk of winding down the war all contributed to my weary mindset at the time.

Charlie Company's next assignment was at a small firebase that was fourteen kilometers west of Tay Ninh City. Rubber plantation workers lived in a village about three klicks away and would visit our garbage dump to sell anything and everything. Our collective fear led many of us to deaden our senses with alcohol, marijuana, hashish, and risky sexual encounters with local prostitutes.

Personally, I embraced weed and hash, but only when safely secure in our firebase and not on guard duty.

My introduction to Vietnamese weed was memorable. In the first few weeks of the tour, I made a trio of friends: Dene from Los Angeles, John from New York and Zeke from Hawaii. We all had in us, a desire to get high and escape Vietnam whenever we could.

On my first trip to the garbage dump with Dene and John, we were offered our first taste of Cambodian Red and I was the first to give it a try. After we ingested some heavy tokes and passed the joint around, the last conscious vision I had was of the assembled group of villagers in the background of our little smoking circle and bright sunlight. When I woke up, I looked up at my two friends and a dozen laughing villagers.

I never passed out again, though not for a lack of trying.

Our search and destroy missions called for a column of us to walk thirteen to eighteen klicks and set up an ambush or a return to the firebase. Sometimes, we had to set out on foot. In other cases, the choppers transported us out to the field and back.

The daily routine for the next three months produced a kind of comfort. We had a typical 25th Infantry company made up of around 25 to 28 men per platoon. Delta platoon was the mortar unit and remained in the firebase for support. Those of us in the other three platoons envied them for most of my tour. Alpha, Bravo, and Charlie platoons went out on search and destroy missions for around twenty five days a month, and rotated ambush duty between them while the other platoons served guard duty at the firebase.

These 'sweeps' varied from day to day. When we woke from a night of little sleep, we'd devour a breakfast of ham and eggs C-Rations while we waited for orders of the day. The first or second lieutenants of each platoon met with the company captain and dished out the orders to squad leaders, who broke the news to the rest of us.

My position was often on point, the lead man in the column when it was our squad's turn. Another position was walking flank, this meant walking about 20 yards to one side of the column, traveling in parallel. I was the skinniest man in my squad, so I couldn't handle carrying ammunition for the M60. Therefore, when walking point I carried a machete, an M16, several clips of ammo, three baseball grenades, a yellow smoke grenade, an entrenching tool, a canteen, some c-rations, a zippo lighter, and cigarettes. When I was on ambush duty, I supplemented this equipment with a trip flare, a Claymore mine, and the necessary wires and blasting caps.

When on point I was typically followed by the lieutenant and the radio operator, unless we had a K9 handler and dog. The lieutenant used his compass and map to direct me across the terrain.

The speed at which the column moved depended on the thickness of the brush in front of us. I was responsible for hacking through the dense thicket and opening a path for those behind me.

The sweeps that started with a chopper ride had an added sense of adventure. The most dangerous 'rides' were when we were dropped into a hot LZ, meaning taking on fire. Door gunners fired almost continuously upon the approach.

On one occasion, we were dropped into some high elephant grass. A soldier in

Bravo company broke a leg and others were hurt in various ways from jumping a distance of ten feet or more with all of their equipment. My jump was less than which allowed me to land somewhat flat-footed, tossed my machete, and roll across the ground. Panic set in when I took too long to locate my machete as the battle raged around me.

On a lighter note, the choppers once dropped us off on the road leading to Camp Bearcat. The mission we were finishing up required quite a bit of equipment. On the road, I was reaching inside the chopper for extra entrenching tools when the pilot decided to set her down, on my right foot! Dene witnessed this odd moment and helped me try to get the door-gunner and pilot's attention. Once the pilot lifted off, Dene laughed so hard he fell back into the ditch.

Thankfully, the rail of the Huey landed on my right foot's baby toe. Once I got my boot off, I discovered that the toe had rolled over and broke from the weight. Dene crawled out of the ditch.

"Are you alright?"

"No... it hurts like hell, but I see you were entertained." I said, trying to smile.

Once we settled into the base, Dene shared the story with our friends, John, Rick, and Zeke.

"We were both screaming and waving at the door gunner and pilots, once the chopper took off, I couldn't stop laughing." Dene said. "Sorry Amigo, it was funny once I found out you were OK."

"It would be cool if you got a Purple Heart out of this, can you picture the home newspaper article?" Zeke said.

Humor was the only therapy we had, and we used it often to keep anyone from freaking out.

When we traveled as a platoon, the

position of point was rotated between the four who were assigned from their squad. On the next sweep, our lieutenant picked me, he mistook my overall sense of panic for alertness. I took note of this and tried to look as tired as the rest of the point men from then on.

When we crossed into the woods on the assigned azimuth, I realized that this forest had many irregular shaped openings that our lieutenant allowed me to transverse without much hacking. We knew that the NVA were in the area, but the first leg of our sweep was uneventful. Once we made the second turn and took a short break, I realized that the day's pattern was going to lead us back to the hot LZ that we left.

The brass in the rear wanted contact.

On the last leg of our sweep, orders came from the rear. We were told to set up ambushes for the night in four different directions. Most of us looked forward to the return of the choppers. The captain was certain that we'd make contact, so he requested a platoon from Bravo company for support. A total of eight squads set up ambushes in and around the whole area. Sergeant Jenkins, our platoon leader, gave out the squad assignments. After that, we all fanned out into two-man teams and positioned ourselves.

As squad leader, Dene picked me to be in his position. While he set some Claymores, I set some trip flares ten yards in front of our position. I was too nervous to get much sleep while I traded guard duty with Dene every two hours.

Ambush duty during a new moon was the absolute worse because of the extreme darkness. It would be a night where we had to rely on our hearing.

At the first hint of daylight, Dene nudged me and asked me what I saw some fifty yards in front of us. It was a couple of Army-issued helmets, not NVA pith helmets! We both realized that one of the squads from Bravo Company had set up their ambush facing us! If either of us had made any noise during the night, we would've engaged in a firefight with our own men. Death by friendly fire had already been added to our fears. It was how Sergeant Mendez found his end.

Fuck.

We move out for another sweep at 10 AM. The first leg took us through some heavy forest, so I felt like my arm was ready to fall off from hacking at the brush. The lieutenant noticed and took me off point for the next two legs of our sweep. Back in the column, I overheard the mumbling of discontent with this operation and the lack of coordination between the platoons. We humped until

5 PM and set ourselves up for dinner and awaited another dreaded night of ambush duty.

As Rick, a dope smoking buddy of ours from Louisiana and I set out our Claymores and trip flares, we had found a sort of cozy ready-made hole that was filled in with heavy grass. I wasn't sure if I would be able to sleep, but at least the ground was soft.

An uncharacteristic breeze and low humidity kept the mosquitoes to a minimum, so I slept during my first two turns. At 4 AM a trip flare went off some thirty yards up the line. In response, Rick fired his M16 while I set off two of our Claymore mines which set off trip flares that lit up the area. Men screamed and tracers from M16s laced about in total chaos as the faint figures scattered in all directions. Rick and I fired our M16s. As the rapid-fire started to die down I heard moaning almost directly under us.

An NVA medic had been torn up by the Claymore mine. He was so disoriented that he crawled into our hole.

"What are we supposed to do with him?" I whispered.

"Let's ask the lieutenant at sunrise." Rick said.

I covered the medic with my poncho and stared into the darkness that had become still. The medic fell quiet an hour later.

At daybreak I told the lieutenant of the body in our position.

"I'll add it to the count for HQ, just get ready to move out." The lieutenant said.

I passed two more NVA bodies on my way back to retrieve my poncho. It had been cast aside and the medic's equipment had been removed by souvenir seekers. My glance at the body was more painful than other enemy dead I had witnessed. I had heard him die.

Seven choppers came later in the morning and carried us back to our firebase. Those same choppers carried two other platoons back to the same area. I heard from others that the captain had been disappointed in the low body count. To Rick and me, the one body count was all we could think about.

When we returned to the base, our platoon was spared from guard duty for one night and was even given the next day off from a sweep. Zeke and John asked me a few times if I wanted to party, but I was sure smoking dope would leave me even more depressed. I was obsessed with thoughts of the medic.

On the following day, we were ordered to patrol in and around the rubber plantations. I was out on point once again, but our surroundings were somewhat comfortable. Our company patrolled these plantations for the next few months without incident.

Our platoon was primarily made up of draftees that were not exactly thrilled to be there. I found myself reminding the men in our platoon that we should not talk about the amazing stretch of time in the rubber plantations. It seemed like bad luck.

My time as point man had its moments. On one sweep I ran into a spider's web that stretched across two rubber trees. As my M16 poked through the enormous web and I immediately backed off. I caught sight of the spider to my left. It was as big as my outstretched hand!

"Let's walk around it," said the lieutenant.

Out of respect for the spider, I thought.

I could see in the web, numerous

insects, bugs and I could swear small birds had a good chance of being caught in it.

My friends and I frequented the garbage dump as often as we could. We smoked dope, laughed at the dumbest stuff, and gave thanks that we hadn't seen the enemy. However, we thought it was strange that the upper brass didn't feel a need to move us into a more hostile area.

We saw ourselves as the protectors of critical assets that were needed on the world market. This was one of our many bullshit sessions, which gradually gave many of us a different worldview that we took back to our divided nation.

One of my favorite full moon nights happened to be when Neil Armstrong made his famous walk on the moon. In a stoner-induced chat between Dene, John, Rick, Zeke and me, we concluded that "the great minds of our country have figured out how to get a man on the moon, yet clueless about how to end this senseless war."

We wondered if more money, soldiers, airstrikes, napalm raids, or B-52 bombings would do the trick, there was no definitive answer. We knew that the war between the North and the South would end someday, but the future of the newly united Vietnam didn't matter anymore.

We just wanted to stay alive and to forget the horrors of combat from a cheap lawn chair, back home.

Dene and Tom – French Fort 1970

CHAPTER 4

STEPPING IN AND OUT

Gentlemen, prepare not to be gone; We have a trifling foolish banquet towards.

William Shakespeare

We all knew that there were areas in the country where one would have no clue there was a war going on. Cam Ranh Bay and our main base at Cu Chi had some of the same amenities that we would find back home such as, warm food at a cafeteria, a recreation area, some stores to buy things, and a movie theater. The area set aside for us at Cu Chi was nicknamed the 'Holiday Inn.' We typically didn't get sent back there unless the brass was getting ready to change our area of operation, or we had been in some intense combat. We were given three days' rest, our weapons taken away from us, and the brass turned a blind eye to what was going on in the barracks.

It was stepping in and out of war.

Our easy patrols in the rubber plantations lasted almost three months. In October of 1969, we returned to Cu Chi and awaited new orders. There was no guard duty or equipment to carry around, so we felt safe enough to let loose and enjoy ourselves.

When we got to our assigned hootchs, groups split up between drinkers, weed smokers, and those soldiers trying their best to keep their nose clean.

Zeke bragged about experiencing over 100 LSD trips at the ripe old age of

19. John, Rick, and I were the most curious about his drug usage. When we knew that we were going to be in the rear for more than a couple days, Zeke would egg us on to give it a try. Zeke's sister, Beverly was living in Hawaii and had sent him a letter with five hits of acid called "Purple Owsley."

"Okay Zeke, let us think about this, maybe I'll consider it tomorrow, let's just go out for some fun tonight," I said.

The first night we were there, I stuck a joint in my pocket and the four of us walked across the huge base camp to the massage parlor. The Army had screened a dozen or so local Vietnamese to work there. When we entered, we would hear a combination of giggling, sighs and, outright moans of pleasure.

The locals loved U.S. dollars, so we paid an admission fee of $2.50, but we soon learned that all of those moans were because of the $2 handjobs. We were able to frequent the massage parlors just often enough to keep us from resorting to the service of prostitutes. I found it extremely sad when we crossed paths with very young boys that pimped out their older sisters.

We found a spot to smoke most of my joint and a fat one that Zeke brought along. The sound of a distant mortar tube and accompanied shouts warned us that a few rounds of mortars were on their way into the camp. The Viet Cong or NVA loved to pop a few rounds into Cu Chi every other night in the hopes of destroying a cargo plane or chopper, but the four of us kept on our appointed mission to the massage parlor.

"Tomorrow's trip is going to change you dudes forever, but don't worry, I'll take good care of all of you." Zeke mused.

After a few hours in the sauna, long shower, a soothing massage with a climactic end, John and I set out to discuss Zeke's plan in private. We came upon what appeared to be an abandoned jeep with the steering wheel secured with a lock and chain. We climbed aboard and joked about driving out west back home to pick up beautiful young girls the Beach Boys sang about.

Out of the darkness, two jeeps came barreling up to us. Two MPs jumped out.

"Get out of the jeep!" one yelled.

"It was locked up when we got here, we were just goofin around." John pleaded.

At the MP station, we were told by a sergeant to empty our pockets. As soon as I flipped out my money, ID card and a small photo of my wife, the sergeant and I found ourselves staring at the remains of a once smoked joint, a cigarette filter and the twisted end with a tiny amount of weed left in it.

"I don't want to see that." the sergeant whispered.

I smiled and slipped the offending item back into my pocket.

After the MPs listened to our story, they called our commander, who was not at all pleased to have his card game interrupted by an MP report on a couple of his knuckleheads. The captain sent his executive officer to retrieve us.

"Cap says you assholes can goof around all you want on shit burning detail for the next two days!" proclaimed the officer.

John and I had the last laugh when it came to shit burning detail. It was the perfect spot to smoke. When we were relieved of this duty around dinner time, Zeke caught up to us in the mess hall line.

He was excited about the little adventure he had planned for us in the evening.

After dinner, we sat around in our hootch, Zeke dumped the acid tabs on the table.

"Take a half a tab to enjoy a nice trip." Zeke said as he cut a tab in half.

John and I looked at each other and then back at Zeke.

"Maybe just a quarter of a tab for our first trip." I said sheepishly.

"You're all crazy, I'll pass." Dene half smiled.

"Yes! This whole place is crazy, give me a half Zeke." Rick interjected.

"Oh amigos, this is going to be some kind of party!" Dene added.

We all took our medicine and watched Zeke take a whole tab.

"Sit back and relax." Zeke slyly smiled.

"Rolling Stone imitators from South Korea are playing at the show hall tonight and I hear they're amazing." Rick said.

Zeke had a huge smile on his face as he waited for a reaction from Rick, John or me. He walked out and came back about fifteen minutes later hiding something behind his back. The next thing we know Zeke tied a wire clothes hanger to the pull chain on our light in the middle of the hootch. He mischievously drapes plastic from the hangar and lit it with his zippo. As the plastic slowly dripped to the ground, we all stared in amazement.

Zeke giggled. He was sure the acid would soon start kicking in. This little show went on for what seemed like forever. We had entered his little alternate universe.

The flaming light show brought in visitors from surrounding barracks. Somebody cranked up some music, fired up a joint, and started a party. Some singing, a little dancing and a lot of bull shit was flying around. I became hyper aware of the blood that was noisily racing through my veins. I was sure it was the effects of the acid. I felt euphorically alive.

The chatter among my comrades felt genuinely clear, even though there were three or four conversations going on at the same time. Then it happened, my mind's eye wandered above all of us and observed the scene. It was a surreal voyage into another level of self-awareness. I wanted the party to last longer, but Rick rallied us around the idea of going to see the Stones imitators.

Everyone slowly wandered out of the hootch and walked across the base to the camouflaged airfield hanger that was used as a show hall.

As we walked along joking for what

seemed like a longer walk than we remembered. Zeke disappeared for some reason and we eventually caught sight of the show hall. We entered some lowland that was underwater. The water was not very deep, but we didn't want to get our boots all muddy. We were about ten or twenty yards from the narrow crossing point when Zeke and our supply sergeant pulled up in a jeep. The jeep made an improvised bridge.

"Climb over my merry comrades!" Zeke proclaimed.

We all climbed over the jeep. Zeke had promised to take care of us. In that weird moment, he did just that.

Once we were inside the hall, more than fifty GIs crowded around to watch the show. The beautiful young Korean women started to play Rolling Stones tunes. It was so realistic that we all got caught up in the show. I was reminded of rock concerts at Cobo Hall in Detroit. It was amazing! After the show, we wandered back towards our hootch, commenting on how incredibly surreal it seemed in the acid glow.

We woke up the next morning being teased by Zeke about us becoming, 'official acid heads.' John would quit after the first trip realizing the stuff was too powerful, he didn't want to push it any further. Rick raved about his trip.

A month later the brass gave us another break. Our company was sent on a three day in-country R&R to Vung Tau, a seaside resort on the South China Sea. When we were there, the Army screened and supplied about one woman for every four GIs. Warm food, a beach and women, this was truly rest and relaxation! John and I gravitated towards a young, fun-loving Cambodian woman who liked smoking dope with us. Sex with her didn't seem appropriate, but that didn't prevent us from commenting on how great her plump, brown breasts were to our hungry eyes. We may have touched her beautiful, smooth brown skin, but the strong weed and hot sun compelled us to sleep more than usual.

On the second day, I asked Zeke if we could try some Purple Owsley again. He told me he'd be glad to be of service and promised to mother any of us who wanted to embark on another trip. As before, I cautiously ate a quarter tab, Rick swallowed a half, and Zeke took a whole tab for himself.

Right on schedule, I started to feel its wonderful effects intensify over my entire body. My pores answered the caressing warmth of the sun. I became totally aware of the inner workings of my heart, lungs, and bloodstream. A gentle sea breeze blew through my hair, and I could feel every little minute trail as it traveled along each hair on my head. A dog emerged from the water and shook itself in rhythmic slow-motion.

Suddenly, I realized that the guys were having tons of fun in the surf with our adopted girlfriend. They coaxed me in. In my state of bliss, I felt as if the ocean was a living being. The sand beneath my feet seemed alive, surrounding my feet and forcefully pulling me out to the sea. I studied how Dene and John caught the waves. Before I knew it I was soaring along on about a three foot wave, it felt like flying, exaggerated tenfold by the effects of the LSD.

We played for what seemed like hours in the sea. I continued to feel the tantalizing effects of the acid, when we were back on the beach. Everything was just about as perfect as it could be.

With just one day left on our in-country R&R, I asked Zeke for one more trip, which would become my short 'acid life' undoing.

"I'm all out of the Purple Owsley, but I have a couple of tabs of Orange Sunshine. It has a much longer lasting effect so we'd have to start early in the morning," Zeke told me.

As with the prior two trips, I asked Zeke to cut a quarter of a tablet for me. Everything I did after that seemed illuminated by Sunshine's strange magical force. The simple act of waving my arm seemed to leave mesmerizing trails of repeating arms. But as the day dredged on, I started to feel agitated and unable to control my thoughts.

"I'm starting to really feel like shit Zeke, what should I do?"

"Smoke some dope dude, you'll wind down quicker," Zeke replied.

After dinner, my friends and some other GIs gathered to share a few joints. One Michigan native serving in the first platoon was boasting about killing an NVA soldier in close combat, the more graphic his story progressed, the more his face became distorted and devilish. I was transfixed on the nastiness and disgusting description of his savage 'heroics' of mutilating an enemy soldier that might have already been deceased. I tried to look away from him.

A force seemed to pull my head back, the man's face became even more distorted and bone-shaking scary.

I felt I was losing my mind as I headed back to the barracks. I wandered into a doorway I thought I was staying in, but it was the wrong one. The occupants stared at me, freaking me out. I bolted from barracks to barracks and started crying loud enough to be heard by everyone in the vicinity. I was approached by our second lieutenant.

"What's the problem Peters?" The

officer asked.

Fortunately, I was making such a commotion that Zeke came over to drag me away from the lieutenant's inquiries.

Zeke found a somewhat remote part of the beach.

"What's going on?" Zeke said as he shook me.

"When is this going to end?" I cried.

"Sunshine acid is laced with amphetamines, sorry this could last maybe two or three more hours." Zeke confessed.

I curled up into a fetal position on the beach and cried for a long time. I was ashamed of taking the acid and was sure I was losing my mind. I had pushed my flight from the horrors of combat too far.

With that said, the incident made me quit taking LSD.

During the night, someone had

mercifully dragged me to my cot. When I woke up, we got ready to leave the area and I joyfully realized that I had my mental facilities back and smiled.

On the week of Christmas 1969, I was on my way to R & R in Hawaii to meet my wife, Pat. A marital reunion and huge step away from the war.

The evening before my flight from Ton Son Nhat airfield to Hawaii, I decided to take in a movie. In the long line to the movie house I spotted a familiar face, a tall Air Force private, John Gaydos. This would mark the second time that I've run into somebody from my hometown in Vietnam. The first time was out in the field. We met up with a mechanize unit, and there stood Dewey Ivy, from Foote Elementary School, in Lincoln Park! To be clear, neither Dewey or John were close friends of mine, but I did know them as classmates and we did get close for those few strange moments. A common bond you never forget, I mean...Holy shit!

Over the years, I would find out John had been killed working at the cheap motel he managed in Melvindale, MI., and Dewey had also died, but I had no details. Sad to realize, they survived Vietnam...but didn't enjoy a long life.

The next morning, I got ready for my flight to see my wife in Hawaii, but I soon discovered my wallet was missing. I thought that I had left it in the shower, it wasn't there so I ran to find the lost and found. I didn't know how my trip would to play out if didn't find my ID and cash.

Luckily, another GI had returned my wallet with my ID and the $450 still in it. I wished that he would have left his name so I could have thanked him. It was an example of how we watched each other's back during the war.

Memories of this week with my new wife in Waikiki, are fuzzy at best.

We stayed at a hotel near the International Marketplace. At one point, we rented a car for a day and drove around the island of Oahu. In the evening we drove to downtown Honolulu to see "Easy Rider". The movie shook me mentally. I may have mentioned my acid adventures to Pat.

As we exited the movie house, we noticed that the interior of our rented Toyota was full of these huge beetles that freaked Pat out. I played the hero and by hand, swept out these crazy looking beetles by hand. Thankfully, they didn't bite.

During the week, our discussions were light and plagued with awkward moments of silence. Pat told me of her brother Gary's return from his tour with the Marines. He was part of the deadly Khe Sanh siege, which killed close to a thousand Marines and between 10,000 and 15,000 North Vietnamese soldiers. If Pat and I actually talked about the war, I would have mentioned that Ho Chi Minh once said: "You can kill 10 of my men for every one I kill of yours, but even at those odds, you will lose and I will win."

We didn't talk about the war. Pat shared one upsetting story with me.

Pat was living with my parents. One day, an official military vehicle pulled up to the front of our house and two uniformed Army personnel made their approach. Pat and my mother thought that I had been killed in action and began sobbing together. The men were actually delivering my Bronze Star and citation. I had told Pat and my mother that I was blessed with a job as a supply clerk and was safe so she didn't have to worry about me. Thanks to these two knuckleheads, the medal cast serious doubt on whether I was a supply clerk. I found out later that I was supposed to approve the delivery of any medals won in the field of battle.

I explained to Pat that this medal was awarded early in my tour, that I was fine now and not to worry about me. But I'm sure she worried anyways. Leaving Pat and returning to the combat zone for five more months made for a depressing flight back to Ton Son Nhat airfield.

To my surprise, the trip to Hawaii would not be my last escape from war. A couple of months after returning from Hawaii, Top, our first sergeant, called both John and I into his office.

"I have two 7 day R&R passes to Hawaii, you guys should go." Top said with a thin lipped smile.

"Thanks Top, we're outta here, when do we leave?" I said.

"Catch a cargo plane tomorrow for Ton Son Nhut, flight to Hawaii leaves the day after." Top said. "Have fun."

"Sure thing Top, thanks!" John said

as we grabbed the paper work.

"Look up my sister, Beverly, when you hit the island." Zeke told us.

We did. Beverly and her friends were wild and free. Though the week seemed like a non-stop party, two memorable occasions stuck with me.

On the second day, I befriended a shy young woman on the beach with Bev's tribe of extroverts. We shared a joint or two and talked all day. That evening, she disappeared. When the rest of us assembled on their communal apartment's huge balcony, Bev felt a need to inform me that Lola, was once Gerald a few years ago. I was confused on one hand, yet fascinated on the other. I asked Bev to elaborate.

"You weren't the least bit suspicious that Lola was the only one of us not wearing a bathing suit?" Bev said.

"Noooo"

I wasn't suspicious and hadn't even considered this, she wore short, cut-off jeans and a flowered, fluffy blouse that exposed her mid-drift that I found sexy.

"Ok, wasn't she totally flat chested?" Bev continued.

"I have just spent many months in South Vietnam where flat-chested women were pretty much the norm." I said.

"Alright, just so you know, Lola has a dick, I just don't want you freaking out and messing up her head any more than it already is!" Bev said staring at me.

Lola never showed up again and it would be more than thirty years before I would meet another transgender woman.

On the third day. I found myself packed into an old Honda Civic with John, Beverly and two of her friends. We drove from Waikiki to the North Shore for a drug deal. The surf on the North Shore was legendary so we spent the afternoon on a beach with surf that was three or four times the size of what I experienced in Vung Tau. I was too high at the time and so were the waves, but I went in anyway. I didn't get by the first wave. I was hit hard and then kept bouncing off the ocean floor in the shallow water till I was eventually washed ashore. It was the most disorientating experience of my young life up until then. John and one of Beverly's friends had to drag me back onto the beach.

After some time to recuperate, John and I sat there laughed hysterically at the idea of dying in Hawaii. Humor served as a mask to hide the sad reality that we might die before we grew old.

It was so incredible and just strange to step in and out of war.

CHAPTER 5

FRENCH FORT

War is not only a matter of equipment, artillery, group troops or air force; it is largely a matter of spirit, or morale.
Chiang Kai-shek

Firebase Santa Barbara, also known as French Fort, was located about ten kilometers to the northeast of Tay Ninh City. It was called French Fort because it had been there since the French War with the Vietnamese. It was like no other firebase that we occupied during my tour. It was extremely well armed and included huge and extremely loud 175mm and 8-inch. artillery guns.

The original fort was square but portions were added later, with very high dirt walls and bunkers that you could walk in and stand up inside. On the four corners, there were flatbed trucks with what was called Quad 50 machine guns mounted on the back pointing outward. Quad 50s were four 50 caliber machine guns that could shoot simultaneously, unbelievable firepower. There was a shower house and mess hall where we would get warm meals most of the time, which was a real luxury compared to the rest of the smaller firebases as we served in.

Our unit was stationed there on two occasions. Initially, we were under the impression that it was a well-fortified and safe. We were surrounded by fields of rice paddies almost as far as you could see, but it wasn't too far from Nui Ba Dinh, also known as the Black Virgin Mountain. The fort could hold more than a whole company and there was a large chopper pad just outside the perimeter. The perimeter was protected by rows and rows of concertina wire, trip flares and Claymore mines. We all felt we could sleep comfortably between guard duties. Platoons took turns venturing outside the fort for sweeps, and occasionally setting up ambushes in the woods to our west.

It was a great place to be on duty. After leaving the fort and changing our A.O. two or three times in the early months of 1970 we found ourselves back at French Fort.

After pulling some pretty rough duty, it was good to be back. We all joked about getting some sleep, a decent shower and some warm food. The first three days were uneventful. Our platoon pulled one sweep of about sixteen kilometers and a night of ambush duty in the rice paddies. One reason to smoke cigarettes was to burn leeches off your legs or other parts of your body from lying in rice paddies overnight.

The unit that was here before us had left quite a mess. We had a problem with rats that we didn't experience in our first stay. How did a kid from Lincoln Park find a way to sleep with rats frequenting his bunker? I kept busy during the day, avoided naps, laid down fully clothed and hoped that I fall fast asleep quickly so if one decides to crawl over me, I don't completely lose it. A fellow from one of the other platoons was disciplined for shooting at a rat, so we had to stick to the ineffective traps that were given to us. My nightmares were worse than the rats themselves.

John and I shared a bunker and on the third night while he was on guard duty, the Quad 50s started firing wildly at about 4 AM. Startled, I jumped up. Some flares floated around outside the perimeter. The mortar platoon started launching rounds that landed 100 yards to the right of our position. The commotion ended about a half-hour later.

I stayed up with John until it was my turn for guard duty at 5 AM. I thought that all would be well. I was wrong.

A huge explosion rocked the whole fort. People yelled that there were sappers and NVA regulars inside the wire which forced us to take up a defensive position. John fired his blooper out one of the fire holes in our bunker, but I stayed at the entrance with my M16 to keep the sappers or regulars away. A second explosion flashed inside the perimeter and temporarily blinded me.

The inside the fort, chaos. Faint figures ran in all directions, smoky tracers ripped across the inner perimeter, the mess hall and ammo dump were on fire.

"Out the front gate! Be quick about it!" Screamed a new staff sergeant.

Rumors began to surface that we were about to be overrun. In a panic, we evacuated French Fort. There was some crossfire, but we couldn't tell where it was coming from. Fortunately, our bunker was set up close to the front entrance so John and I were some of the first GIs to get out of the besieged fort.

When another large explosion rocked the area, I noticed that a Cobra gunship and at least one fighter jet were providing support. I was scared shitless, but the direction that I was running in seemed relatively safe. The Cobra unleased sporadic mini gun bursts on the far side of the fort. Seconds later, the jet dropped a bomb just outside our west perimeter. After that, our bunker took a direct hit from an incoming mortar.

We knew that we were sitting ducks out there because most of us had just grabbed a weapon and a bandolier.

"You men head out around to cut off the enemy!" A sergeant suggested.

The sergeant then noticed we weren't well-armed, and some GIs were without boots.

"Never mind, stay put."

After about two hours of air, mortar, and artillery fire, things died down to an uncomfortable stillness. However, French Fort was a disaster. When we returned to the fort, we found a 50-foot wide bomb crater where the ammo supply dump used to be. On top of that, the mess hall was destroyed and two perimeter bunkers suffered heavy mortar damage. One of them was ours.

To make matters worse, we never heard an official body count report. It was bad for morale.

Over the next two weeks, we rebuilt the fort with the help of a crew from the Army's 18th Engineer Brigade.

CHAPTER 6

AL KALINE IN SOUTH VIETNAM

*There's a scent and special kind of air
in the old Tiger stadium sitting with my Dad
watching in awe as Kaline throws a tightrope
strike from the warning path to home plate*

A few weeks later, we were
relocated to a new firebase closer to the
Cambodian border. After we completed
our first daytime sweep, we settled in a
secure wood line for a dinner of C rations.
The lieutenant, the radioman, Mike, and
Rick set out to find a good ambush site
for the night. I was left behind with Nisbit,
Lawrence "Don't-call-me-Larry" on the
machine gun, and two new guys. We had

walked across a long trail in an open field of waist-high elephant grass, quietly wishing that we were in one of the other three squads from our platoon. They traveled back to the firebase.

Nisbit and I had the most experience of the men sitting around, Lawrence always acted kind of gung ho, but he hadn't been in a firefight yet, and the two new guys had only been in the field for a few weeks.

Nisbit was a good-natured Jamaican fellow from Chicago.

"I've gotten some street smarts from Chicago, but the American Dream is nowhere to be found." He admitted.

We reminisced and laughed as I leaned against a tree. All of a sudden, his eyes went wide. I immediately scrambled for my M16 and motioned for the others to stay down. As I peeked around the tree, I saw a line of NVA regulars walking up the same path that we had just used an hour or so earlier. I quietly motioned for Lawrence to set up the M60 and ordered the two new guys to be ready to shoot if we're overrun but don't spray shots towards us. One tree and a shallow hole was the only cover that Nisbit and I had at our disposal, but the others were able to duck behind some trees and bushes.

Nisbit had an M79 blooper, I told him that I was going to open up on point man. When they retreated, he could launch some grenades out onto the field. I whispered to Lawrence I didn't want him to fire until I fired first.

When I peeked around the tree, the point man in the column was close. I noticed that he was joking with his comrade behind him. I couldn't believe he didn't smell us and his happy spirits.

Experience told me to wait until I

was sure that I could stop the column by shooting the point man. As the seconds ticked away, we kept quiet. When the point man noticed the wood line in front of him, I opened fire. The burst knocked him back. I was not sure if the second soldier was hit, but he fell as well and all hell broke loose.

Nisbit launched a grenade. I emptied my magazine in the general area of the path. When I reloaded my weapon, Lawrence had his head down, I couldn't tell if he was taking fire, but he was being useless at the moment that we really needed him. I flipped back around and sprayed three short bursts, and then emptied my second magazine. Nisbit fired a few more grenades out into the open field and adjacent wood line.

I didn't think that we were taking fire, so I got a baseball grenade, flipped off the safety clip, pulled the pin and pretended that I was Al Kaline firing from deep right field to home at Tiger Stadium. I was pleased with the results and wanted to celebrate. However...

Seconds later, a grenade careened off a tree and fell ten feet in front of us. We dove into our hole before it went off.

It was obvious that one of the new guys had tried to throw a grenade, but it hit a tree in front of them, and almost killed Nisbit and me.

I crawled towards Lawrence.

"Why weren't you firing!" I screamed.

"They had me pinned down man." Lawrence whined.

"Asshole." I mumbled and crawled back to my position.

I was convinced that the NVA had dragged their wounded back across the field back into the thick forest.

Moments later, I heard a chopper.

The trees around us prevented me from seeing where it was, but the long burst of a minigun too close to our position told me that it was a Cobra firing on us. I pulled the pin on a yellow smoke grenade, threw it out in front of the trees, and told everybody to retreat into the woods.

When things quieted down, the gunship left and we crawled our way back to our original position. A short while later, the lieutenant, Rick, and Mike showed up.

"Wow, my first firefight!" Lawrence bragged.

Nisbit and I kept the truth to ourselves. The lieutenant suggested that we should go back out on the trail and see if we had a body count. Rick, Nisbit and I set out for the field.

In all of my combat experiences, my first firefight haunted me profoundly. My mind split between soldier and killer.

On the trail, I noticed there were blood trails that led back up the path. I was quietly pleased that we did not find a body.

"I'm glad you guys are all right," the lieutenant said.

That became a sort of turning point between me and our West Point educated Lt. Reese. I was sure he was going to mimic the body count obsession we usually heard from the brass. I realized that front line officers did empathize with us from time to time. I needed it this time.

CHAPTER 7

CAMBODIA

The Navy fed us delicious meals before going out on ambush maneuvers on Cambodian border. We joked that if we were killed at least we had a nice warm meal in our bellies.

In February of 1970, I was excited about getting a job in Cu Chi. A treasured unwritten courtesy in the 25th Infantry was that they tried to find a job in our main basecamp for combat tired short-timers with less than 100 days left of their tour. It seemed like every discussion with other GIs centered around becoming a short timer and making it home alive. I hadn't heard anything so I talked about it with Top, our Master Sergeant.

"Did you talk to the XO about a rear job for me Top?" I asked.

"Don't get your hopes up kid, rumors have it that something big is coming down." Top replied.

The "something big" presented itself in late April of 1970. President Richard Nixon authorized the withdrawal of 150,000 U.S. troops in an effort to carry out his Vietnamization of the war. At the same time, South Vietnamese forces were sent into Cambodia.

On May 1st, Nixon included U.S. forces in the Cambodian Invasion. Our 25th Infantry was to join forces with the 1st Cavalry and invade the border west of Tay Ninh.

The unwritten courtesies of our unit were off the table. We had to serve in the field until four days before our return home.

Our unit moved around a lot

between February of 1970 and the end of my tour. We teamed up with a small mechanized unit from the 1st Cavalry and spent some weeks in maneuvers and sweeps in an area that we weren't too familiar with to the east and south of Tay Ninh.

We took over an area after the Big Red One pulled out of South Vietnam. The 1st Infantry Division's large basecamp in the area was Camp Bearcat. The labor-intensive set up of small temporary camps on the hard red clay around Bearcat felt like busywork to most of us. We would dig holes, fill sand bags and set up a perimeter, only to move a week later and start over again at a new location. The good news was that we weren't making much contact with the NVA or the Viet Cong.

As a short-timer, I found ways to get out of the field. One painful way was to ask to see the dentist in Cu Chi. I was not sure how they were treating basecamp warriors and officers, but I do know that foot soldiers coming in from the field were not given the benefit of fillings or root canals. On two separate occasions the dentist in Cu Chi removed molars that were bothering me.

Today, I have a large gap on the lower left side of my teeth because of these visits. It was called "sham time", which was considered a cowardly act by sergeants and officers if the reasons seemed frivolous. We didn't care. It only meant that they were one-day closer to getting out of the country alive.

At one point, I volunteered for sniper school which resulted in a three-day training in Bien Hoa. We trained on an M14 with a high-powered scope. I got impressive compliments from my instructors, but the brass never used me as a sniper. I considered it good sham time, three days closer to my DEROS.

By far, the oddest sham time I received was being pulled out of the field of combat by the Criminal Investigation Department of the Army (CID).

In early 1970. I was ordered to meet with two Army CID personnel in Cu Chi with no rank insignia on their uniforms. Like a weird dream, I found myself being interrogated in a bare hootch. They made vague references to my feelings about the war. When I returned vague answers, I realized that a sham time opportunity was being handed to me on a platter.

The questioning went on for hours, but I couldn't quite figure out how much trouble I was really in until I insisted on knowing why I was there.

"You signed a petition, 'GIs United Against the War in Vietnam,'" one of them finally admitted.

Great! They have the wrong Tom Peters. I thought.

"And where was I when I signed this petition?" I asked.

"Fort Benning, Georgia"

"So what if I did?"

That smart-ass remark abruptly triggered anger. The questioner intensified the line of questioning.

I raised my voice in a weird protest.

"You order me out of the field and put me through this crap about a signature I supposedly signed at Fort Benning, where I've never been in my life!" I exclaimed.

The hour was getting late, so I was told I'd be confined to my quarters with an MP at the door for the night.

As I tried to fall asleep, I wondered if this was sham time that I could possibly milk another day without serious consequences, or have I said enough to land myself in the brig.

Morning in Cu Chi brought another hot, muggy day. Our platoon returned for some much needed rest. When a few buddies entered the barracks they joked about the MP at the door.

"You get busted Peters or do MPs protect short-timers these days?"

"Couple of CID dudes think I'm against this war." I smiled even though I was instructed not to talk about it.

"Peters, get your ass out here!" Lt. Reese screamed. "Are you a fucking commie Peters?"

"No Sir!" I reply.

"Next time you folks pull one of my men out of the fucking field, you'd better have some solid evidence! Peters is going out with us on a sweep near the border tomorrow morning. You're both welcome to join us or close the case!"

I was sure that he was bluffing, but the CID fellas walked away with Reese to the command center. I never saw them again. Later, Reese instructed me to keep the whole screwed up affair to myself.

After that strange incident, we worked with the U.S. Navy to obtain transport up and down the Song Vam Do Dong river near the Cambodian border. These were scary operations because the river patrol boats we rode in to ambush sites were sitting ducks for RPGs.

However, the Navy fed us warm, delicious meals before we went out on these ambush maneuvers. Dene, John and I often joked that if we were killed at least we had a nice warm meal in our bellies.

All of the limited action that we would see in the spring of 1970, came to an end on April 30th as a huge clumsy force of two regiments from the 5th and 25th Infantry, two squadrons of armored support, and three Ranger battalions would joined the 8700 ARVN troops in an operation called, Toan Thang 42.

The invasion of Cambodia was on.

The very next day, the US launched a B-52 bomber raid in the area, dropping 775 tons of explosives deep in the area just west of us.

The grand prize the generals were looking for was the Central Office of South Vietnam (COSVN). This was supposed to be the center of all operations for the North Vietnamese in South Vietnam. It was never found, but not for a lack of trying. Most of the NVA and Viet Cong had moved west into Cambodia early in the operations.

We all knew that large forces had been taking sanctuary in Cambodia for years. I kept a low profile because I had thirty days left in my tour. I got a letter from Dene. He joked that he had been put in charge of an armored unit in Ft. Hood,

Texas. In his letter, he urged me to hang in there because he knew my time was getting short. We all knew, we were most vulnerable as newbies and short-timers.

That vulnerability showed itself during a reconnaissance operation I was on that was supposed to be putting us out ahead of some straggling NVA troops that were moving west. We had a relatively new lieutenant and troops that had been in country for some time, but hadn't seen much action. A gung-ho sergeant that I wasn't too fond of took point position. I followed right behind the radio man concerned that the lieutenant might lead us into an ambush. The sergeant wanted to take a road, but I urged the lieutenant not to listen to him.

"Mind your own business asshole." the sergeant said.

"I have only 18 days left, give me a break Sergeant." I replied.

"Hand me the machete and take a break!" I said, staring a hole through him.

There was some serious rage in my voice. I got my way.

As we advanced through the thick forest I noticed that we were walking parallel to a slightly raised ridge line to our left. The hair on the back of my neck signaled ambush, so I eased off our set azimuth and veered to the right.

The lieutenant kept correcting me, but this where my memory fails me, I know that there was strong arguing between the lieutenant, sergeant and myself. There were bunkers involved, and threats made over whether to attack or call for artillery.

The friction must have put me over the edge mentally. Four days later, I got on a resupply chopper, and went back to Cu Chi. AWOL, Absent without official leave.

CHAPTER 8

PATRIOTISM OR TREASON

The difference between treason and patriotism is only a matter of dates.

Alexandre Dumas

When the resupply chopper landed in Cu Chi, I reported to our XO, First Lieutenant Harry Morris. He was a concerned that I had left the field early, but he told me not to worry about it. After I checked in my weapon and ammunition he directed me to a hootch. I was told to rest and wait.

I was quite nervous. The captain could have been angry enough to court-martial me for leaving the field without permission. My actions in the last week had been confrontational, but I was glad to be able to sleep for over 12 full hours, until the following morning.

After breakfast, I asked Lt. Morris.

"Sir, will it be alright if I just hang out until the paperwork is all in order to be able to leave to go home?"

"I'm going to assume your captain is far too busy to pursue a court-martial on a decorated soldier with over 350 days in country. Let's just see what happens. I'm sure it will be fine, relax and let me handle it."

Lt. Morris shined in my eyes, much like Lt. Reese. I admired both of these officers' kindness they had shown me under strange circumstances. Morris's humanity lifted my heart at a critical time when I was scared to death of being court-martialed. This kind, caring encouragement, put me in a good enough mood to go to the PX to purchase gifts to bring home and spent some leisurely time just walking around the base.

When I got back, Lt. Morris gave me the news that two GIs from our weapons platoon, Sergeant Bill Airlee and Specialist 4 Billy Ray Parker were killed in action.

Were my actions in the field in those last few weeks the mark of a coward? I don't remember it well, which raises many questions about the integrity of all my actions during the Cambodian invasion.

I thought about Bill and Billy's deaths. How ironic it was that most of us grunts envied the weapons platoon folks because they mainly stayed back in our firebases for support. For the invasion, they were given weapons and ordered to join us in the field. They were so close to the end of their tour, so close.

I was supposed to be happy that my tour was almost over, but I couldn't shake the feeling that I had let down my fellow GIs. I was thankful that the few comrades that were hanging around in my last days were not dope smokers. Getting high would have made me even more depressed. Weed never fixed head-wrenching things. It just quieted the doubts and demons enough to rest. I was exhausted enough to sleep for a week.

Lt. Morris may have sensed my depression. He'd stop by the barracks occasionally and found me on my cot.

"How are you doing Peters? Paperwork is moving along and no word from your captain," he said reassuringly.

Bless his heart, it did help, but I wasn't excited or happy about leaving.

With two days left in my tour the lieutenant entered my barracks with a smile and an envelope.

"All your papers are in order and a cargo plane leaves in the morning for Ton Son Nhat airport," he said.

"Thank you sir! But cargo planes make me nervous. Maybe I'll just get a ride on a truck into Saigon." I replied.

Lt. Morris looked at me kind of funny for a moment.

"Are you serious?"

"Is it possible?" I asked.

"I'd pick the flight over the road to Saigon. I'll just say goodbye and good luck," as he shook my hand.

He smiled and handed over my paperwork for processing at Camp Alpha in Saigon.

CHAPTER 9

RETURNING HOME

When my flight landed in Oakland, California, I chimed in with everybody else and kissed the ground.

The trip to Saigon was more adventurous than I needed it to be. After purchasing a suitcase for gifts and packing my duffel bag, I headed out to the entrance of the Cu Chi base. I caught the attention of the driver of an Army truck.

"Are you headed to Saigon? I need to get to the airport."

"Sure, jump in."

Everything up to that moment seemed quite normal. When he hit the accelerator, my head flipped back and my heart raced. *Great, a crazy GI.* I thought.

To be fair, it seemed like everybody drove insanely wild on South Vietnamese roads. It was all new to me, I hadn't spent much time on the roads and highways.

Hordes of small motorbikes, a few cars, and a variety of military vehicles sped in all directions. Everyone drove as fast as they possibly could, as if they hoped to outrun a mortar shell or stray bullet.

What the fuck? I thought. *I spent a whole year here and now I'm gonna die with just a couple days left at the hands of this maniac.*

At one point, the driver avoided a head-on collision with a motorbike, by cutting in front of a large military truck filled with ARVN troops. The truck veered off the road and struck a food stand. Two of the ARVN soldiers retaliated by shooting at us, so I curled up on the floorboard.

"You're gonna get me killed." I screamed. "Get me out of here!"

The driver just laughed and drove on. I bounced around until he had to stop because of heavy traffic. I wanted to strangle him, but he was a big guy and quite insane judging by the look on his face. I contemplated getting out of the truck, but my bags were in the back.

We made it to the airport in record time.

The TWA flight was uneventful and its crew was attentive and pleasant. We were all too excited to sleep on the long flight. When the jet landed in Oakland, California, I chimed in with everybody else and kissed the ground.

My younger brothers didn't appreciate my decision to throw away my jungle fatigues and boots in the nearest restroom. I put on my dress greens. Those battle clothes had to go... I was out of the war.

After thirty wonderful days in Michigan visiting family and friends, Pat and I packed up a small trailer and hitched it to our car and headed to Fort Campbell, Kentucky. Once we arrived, we were told that I was supposed to be in Fort Carson, Colorado. So, we headed west.

We rented a furnished apartment in Colorado Springs and struck up a friendship with another Vietnam vet and his wife next door. The man packed his huge imported Sansai speakers with Vietnamese weed. We became smoking buddies.

At Fort Carson, I fell into a bizarre duty pattern. I drove to the fort at 6 AM for "Reveille," but was told that I didn't need the classes offered, so I was allowed to return to our apartment off-base after some small cleaning detail.

In July and August of 1970 it seemed like I was having the time of my life. However, tragedy struck when of my dear cousin, Duane Riley, was killed in an automobile accident near Fort Hood, Texas. Death didn't wait to visit this young man that may have eventually been deployed to Vietnam, it caught up with him on the way. I spent a couple of summers with the Riley family, Duane and his brother Dale were close to my age.

To add to that pain, my younger brother David, was almost killed in a car accident on his way back from Woodstock. A friend of his was killed. I hoped that Dave would draw a high number in the new draft lottery and be safe from the insanity of this war. Yet in an instant, he was laid up in an Albany hospital for weeks.

September rolled around, I was told by the brass at Fort Carson I could get out of the Army early if I applied for college, so I enrolled at Henry Ford Community College. After some paperwork, my wife and I were on the road back to Michigan.

CHAPTER 10

RAISING A FAMILY AND GREAT LAKES STEEL

I knew I'd become a more complete person
Maybe that's what dreamers seek

To the workers at the steel mill, it was as if nothing had happened, but the change in me wouldn't surface for years.

Since I worked for more than a year in a union shop, my seniority at the steel mill carried on from my time in military service. I now had three and a half years of precious seniority.

I worked in the open hearth furnaces in the fall of 1967 before I was drafted. From the floor, the open hearth, with men shoveling ingredients into these doorways that were spewing hot gases and steam from the molten steel, it looked like a scene from what most of us would imagine hell looks like. It took eight hours to yield the 250-ton ladle full of molten steel at 2,900 degrees.

These relics of the past were being torn down now and replaced with a new steel making process. The basic oxygen plant (BOP) was a game changer for the steel industry in the 1970s. The BOPs processing time for a ladle full of molten steel compared to the open hearth went from 8 hours to about 23 minutes!

What interested me at the time was the gigantic overhead cranes that handled ladles and buckets with spouts that poured the pig iron and scrap into the BOP vessel, called the hot metal cranes. After a sustained air/oxygen blast, the ingredients reached 2,900 degrees and became steel, the vessel was tilted the opposite way and the molten steel was poured into ladles. Ladle cranes picked up these ladles and poured the steel into molds. An extremely dangerous process.

I set my sights on the big cranes. It would take more than ten years running smaller overhead cranes in other buildings before I had enough seniority to land a hot metal crane job.

It was hazardous work anywhere around the BOP, but myself and a couple veteran friends felt drawn to the most dangerous and thrilling jobs in the mill.

During that ten years, the ebbs and tides of the economy meant that I had to be cut back or demoted to various undesirable jobs throughout the mill.

My work as a bricklayer helper was the most challenging job of all. One could easily fit a small house inside one of the two side by side vessels erected to make steel at our mill. One vessel would remain operational while another would be 'cooled off' to about 110 degrees to have the interior heat-resistant brick liner replaced. As a helper, I carried 30 pound, 36 inch bricks one by one from the temporary elevator in the middle of the vessel to wherever the bricklayer told us to set it down. In the extreme heat and strenuous nature of the work, we had breaks every half hour, thanks to the union, a phrase I never use enough.

The steel mill stretched for about a mile along the Detroit River. Zug Island was on the northern end. My older daughter Jeannie and her husband Bryan have worked there for many years. The ships from Upper Michigan dropped off the iron ore pellets, then processed in the island's blast furnaces to make pig iron for steel making. A quarter mile south of the island, there's a complex called the 80" mill where thick slabs were turned into coils of steel, mainly for the auto industry. There were coil processing and maintenance buildings all along the river with many train tracks for moving materials and equipment. My father worked for over 25 years on the railroad at the mill. I was pleased when he was finally able to retire.

The fact that I was going to night school at Wayne State University and looked like a hippie alienated me from most of the older steelworkers.

The older workers genuinely thought that they had the good life, so it seemed like an insult to their lifestyle to go to college. They would joke about how dumb a certain supervisor was and blamed it on being college educated. Fortunately, my friends understood my quest for a better life, after the steel mill.

Pat and I lived in a tiny apartment across from the Detroit River, with a shared bathroom, for $50 a month. We would need a bigger apartment towards the end the following year with the arrival of our first son, Christopher. Chris was the first grandson on either side of the family so it was fun to see him get plenty of attention. I always felt like I didn't give him enough of my time, given the long hours that I was putting in at work and classes at college.

It was difficult for Pat to get pregnant, but she was determined. Five years later, our daughter Jeannie was born. Jeannie quickly became the niece and granddaughter everyone wanted to hold and care for.

Justin was born a little more than a year later. We all lived in the two story home on Warwick Street for about thirteen memorable years.

Our three youngsters became a common site on Warwick. Chris always stuck up for his younger siblings and led the way in T-ball and Little League. Jeannie mothered the younger kids on the block as she dragged her Raggedy Ann doll for comfort and liked to help Pat and me with chores and projects. Justin was a joy as well, always entertaining all of us and kept the general mood light and fun.

Eventually, I worked my way up to a ladle crane job, I started pressing the envelope in other areas. I became active within the union as a shop steward.

The electricians had a shop to socialize in. On my breaks, I'd visit the shops were conversations were a rich mixture of mill talk, childish teasing, and present-day culture and politics.

Ladle crane operators were known for their courage during what was innocently called a 'runner'. When a ladle of molten steel was positioned over the cast iron molds, a steel pourer on a dangerous platform pushed down on a long lever to open a stream of molten steel into a mold. On rail tracks about 15 molds were lined up to complete the pour. A runner occurred once every three months or so when the steel pourer's lever would malfunction causing the stream not to stop between molds. The ladle crane operator was on his own at that point. All workers in the area would scream "RUNNER!" and flee the platform. Imagine molten steel at 2,900 degrees flying everywhere as the operator moved the steady pouring ladle from mold to mold until the ladle was empty.

I poured several runners over my ladle crane years, an adrenaline filled experience not unlike combat.

Safety at the mill was always a big issue. I learned that lip service to safety issues was commonplace. Workers were killed or maimed on the job in almost every other year I worked at the mill.

My father told me this story more than a few times, I was convinced it traumatized him. A railroad worker was impaled by the couplings connecting two rail cars. While conscious and in shock, supervisors immediately summoned his wife. She got to the scene in time to say goodbye to her husband. Medical personnel on the scene warned the decoupling of the two railroad cars would probably kill him. It did.

Naturally, many fellow workers had stories as well. I was present during three separate gruesome deaths. If you're squeamish, skip the next three paragraphs.

Crane operators and maintenance workers would often walk the crane runway near the top of each building. The clearance between the huge building Ibeams and the gigantic overhead cranes was sometimes less than a foot. Walking these runways meant you had to time yourself carefully, going around a beam to avoid the moving cranes. On one of my shifts, an electrician was 'rolled', as the old-timers called it, another words the moving crane pinned him against the I-beam and killed on the spot.

On another occasion when I was on an adjacent hot metal crane, molten pig iron was what we called 'burped' out onto the floor in front of the vessel. A worker was trapped and burned alive.

Lastly, the most gruesome, happened to a 'scrap-baller', a job I once was demoted to during a cut back. Strips of razor sharp slices, about an inch wide, are trimmed off a coil of steel at a very fast pace. The trim was wrapped around a thick horizontal pole which was meant to spin at the same rate as the coil of steel. A scrap-baller was present to shut things down if this rate got screwed up and a ribbon of trimmed steel would fly everywhere. While rewinding a floor full of trim, the scrap-baller was knocked down to his hands and knees, trim suddenly wrapped around his head and pulled tight, decapitating him.

A co-worker would be killed in such a gruesome manner and I wouldn't be able to find an article in the Detroit News or Detroit Free Press. The front page news would often be about a drive-by shooting on the east side. At newspaper board meetings, I imagine the discussions about 'not scaring the workers making our steel and cars' yet feasting on gun and drug violence in the poor black neighborhoods of the city.

I don't recall those articles addressing extreme poverty, racism, and disenfranchisement. Only an occasionally opinion column in the Detroit Free Press.

On the environmental side of things, steel mills release a large amount of particles into the air. As a child, it was generally accepted that the smoke coming from the stacks meant jobs, not pollution. The 60s and 70s brought the environmental movement and the invention of the precipitator for the steel mill. It worked by collecting particles onto charged plates from a high-voltage electrostatic charge.

When the precipitator worked correctly, only clean steam would leave the stack. However, the precipitator could only collect a certain volume of particles over a given time. A time that didn't fit production demands.

When I poured the pig iron into the vessel to reach production timelines, the result overwhelmed the precipitator and allowed vast amounts of pollutants into the air. The average pour was a little less than a minute long.

The Environmental Protection Agency (EPA) inspectors told steel executives when they were coming in for an inspection. During EPA's annual inspection, supervisors told us to pour the pig iron over the course of twenty minutes instead of one. The inspector would then give the steel mill a clean bill of health.

I fear this was done all over the country.

By this time, I was convinced the power and destruction I saw in Vietnam, was created by the same men that yielded power in my country. These powerful men's victims were the people of my country.

In 1980, I was diagnosed with acromegaly, a tumor on my pituitary gland that needed to be removed. Dr. Chandler from the University of Michigan Hospital gave me a successful operation which made me feel thankful for my physical health and modern healthcare. However, I couldn't dodge bouts of depression.

In my stash of thousands of black and white negatives, I put two of them together and superimposed them. One self-portrait of me, a distraught, disheveled Jesus Christ look-alike, pathetically stoned was superimposed over a photo of a Southfield Road underpass on my way to work. It was a scene in my head repeated on many days driving into the steel mill. I thought about how easy it would be to pull into the middle embankment and end it all. Luckily, I sought out help. Thoughts of my children kept me in the correct lane during those dark periods of time.

Unfortunately, it had been too late for my marriage. In 1984, Pat and I got divorced. I didn't work hard enough on our marriage.

Pat and I treated each other with respect throughout the years. After the divorce, Pat married Dave and I married Carol 'on the rebound' as they say. Before the end of our honeymoon, I sensed that I had rushed in and made a mistake. With stubborn denial that I could had blown another marriage, I hung in there. Six years later, I file for a divorced a second time.

In the early 1990s, I was paying child support to Pat and alimony to Carol. To make more money, I became an electrician and started an electrical contracting company called Alva Electric. I could clear almost $300 on most Saturday mornings doing a somewhat dangerous service change on a house, handling electrified wires to re-wire the incoming line and meter, plus install new circuit-breaker panels.

A less dangerous and fun sideline was wedding photography on Saturday evenings for similar profit. All in an effort to make ends meet.

With that said, my unmarried status and weekend custody of the children gave me time to finish my undergrad work and start on my Master's degree.

Chris, Jeannie, and Justin were warm and sweet throughout this whole time, instinctively knowing when to give me space, and when they or I needed a hug. They became my moral compass, and I drove forward with my dream of leaving the steel mill and moving out west with at least a higher degree.

Thanks to the kindness of my close friend from high school, Tom Walsh, I fell in love with Southern California. I spent vacations at his place on a hill in Orange, California. Tom and his wife, Barb let me sleep on the couch and loaned me one of their Mercedes. I drove the coast, to Laguna Beach, Topanga, Ventura and all areas of L.A., declared it to be my future someday... my paradise!

On one trip, Tom met with a friend that was seeking financial advice. The friend explained that he had just spent five months on a fishing vessel in the Bering Straits and made $54,000. I was fascinated and pressed for more information. The friend told me that it was extremely hard work on treacherous seas, but I was focused on the huge amount of money for what I was considering a short period of time.

Another time, an older couple took a liking to me and asked me to come to their ranch in Alberta, Canada to help manage it for a salary and free room and board.

I never acted on these adventures.

It takes a strong, persistent, emotional, and selfish pull, to move away from one's family. I had that pull for many years. I knew I'd become a more complete person. Maybe that's what dreamers seek.

CHAPTER 11

A NEW LIFE IN THE WEST

JoAn and I met for lunch in Marina Del Rey, which changed everything.

I moved in with my parents in February 1997, as I prepared to retire from the steel mill in mid-July of that year. My father was very ill. I hadn't realized how bad my father's lungs had deteriorated. The coughing spells made it obvious to me he wasn't going to live to see the end of the year. My father passed away in late March.

When I arrived at Wyandotte Hospital, the site of my deceased father planted itself in my memory. His breathless mouth was wide opened in a similar way of the dead that I had often encountered in South Vietnam.

After suffering through the funeral, my mother and I had a talk about my plans to move out west in late July. Mom mentioned to me that she was surrounded by plenty of sons and daughters that would take care of her and that I should follow my dreams.

I did. After I signed my retirement papers, I hooked a trailer to my car, packed my things, and set out for Phoenix, Arizona.

The single life that I enjoyed in Michigan in the mid-1990s was just a prelude to what I would encountered out west.

I found a job as a graphic designer in Phoenix. You may be wondering where that came from, but I had been working with computers since 1985. It wasn't all that difficult in my mind.

Working the night shift, I settled into a small apartment on Thunderbird Road on the north end of Phoenix. The swimming pool in the complex appeared to be made just for me, because nobody else used it. It didn't take me long to discover the nightlife in Scottsdale. The weekends were amazing and I had a series of curious, yet interesting relationships.

On one occasion, I put my belongings in storage and moved in with, first, a wealthy woman who had recently divorced. The husband kept the house in Florence, Italy and she got the gigantic house in Scottsdale.

She had a PhD in philosophy and a magnificent collection of books in her study. When it seemed evident that the relationship wasn't going to last, I asked her if there was one book on philosophy

she would recommend. She handed me a
copy of "Letters from a Stoic" by Seneca.
This book became one I would recommend
to anyone dipping their toes in the murky
waters of philosophy. Seneca's validation
of all religions resonated with me.

On the second go around, I dated a
woman who owned a company that
hosted tours of Kenya and lived in an old
famous cowboy author's former house in
Cave Creek, Arizona.

Once this relationship ended, I quit
my job to head to Southern California.

I had an appointment to take a test
for another graphic designer position in
Van Nuys, CA. I thought I did well, but
afterwards, the man in charge said that
he would call in two weeks if the company
had an open position. As the other
applicants were shuffling out, I pulled the
man over to the window overlooking the
parking lot.

"Please sir, notice that car with the trailer hooked up to it down there, it's mine. I worked for a year as a graphic designer in Phoenix. Would you please consider hiring me?" I said.

The man disappeared, then came down the hall with one of the owner's.

"I'm told your anxious to go to work, that true?"

"Yes sir, I've been working with computers since 1985, I just worked as a graphic designer for a year in Phoenix and I'm sure I have a better work ethic than any of those kids I was testing with." I pleaded.

He gave me the job. I pulled out of the parking lot and drove across Sepulveda Boulevard to a small complex, and moved right into a cheap studio apartment.

In less than a year, I rose to the highest level they had, which gave me a chance to work on ads for the Los Angeles Times, Daily News, and the Daily Breeze. The company took work from all of the major newspapers in L.A. after they eliminated their graphic design departments. It was appropriately named, Ad-Out. Outsourcing was responsible for the loss of many union jobs.

Still, a job was a job, I had a lot of with Ria Snow and graphic designers on the nightshift.

Two incredible things happened during this time. I found a three outrageous teaching positions, a tenured professor position and my future wife.

My first teaching position came about from Internet job postings. I got a call from Program Director at the Art Institute of Los Angeles just after New Year's Day, 1999.

"I need a Typography instructor, can you teach typography?" She asked.

"Of course, when do you want me to start?" I replied.

"Next Monday, I believe it's the 11th. I have all the materials you need."

How does the saying go? *'Fake it til you make it.'* I couldn't believe I was teaching in L.A. for $45 an hour.

Later I was offered an opportunity to teach a Mac Illustration course at the UCLA extension school. I thought that my $50 an hour wage was a lot until I did all the prep work and taught the four hour class on Monday nights.

The class of fifteen students didn't sit at computers unless they brought their own. When the student evaluations came in, most students were pissed off about not having a computer lab. The low ratings meant I only lasted one semester.

After that, I taught and coordinated the technical program at Los Angeles ORT Technical Institute.

Although I didn't know it at the time, I had to deal with a lot of students with learning disabilities.

Bless my mother's heart, no matter how many jobs I told her about, she boasted to her friends that her oldest son was teaching at UCLA.

While I was still at Ad-Out, I met JoAn Joseph at the Century Club in Century City. It was an exec's birthday party and what a night.

At the time, the club was a multistage, multilevel dance hall with disco on some stages, hard rock on others, and reggae on the patio. When I caught a glimpse of JoAn, she was peering over the railing down at a fashion show set to disco music. She turned to look at me, our eyes met, and I approached her. We talked for quite a while. Talking led to dancing.

We danced until the party was over.

I knew that we had some magic going on between us.

As we walked to the parking lot to go to the after party, I kissed her shoulder. Her scent was intoxicating.

The get together in West L.A. lasted all night. At 5AM, a couple asked us how long we had been together. We both laughed.

"About eight hours," we said.

We started dating and spent cozy evenings in my 235 square-foot studio, near Venice Beach. We called it the 'hallway.' When my futon was extended to make a queen-size bed, you had to crawl over it to get to the tiny kitchen or bathroom.

JoAn had a larger one-bedroom apartment in West L.A., so it wasn't long until I moved in with her.

JoAn and I thrived through this period. However, my family was not aware that she was African-American. I had dated white, black, Hispanic, Asian, and trans sexual women during my 12 years of singlehood, so diversity wasn't new for me. However, I anticipated it would be challenging to bring her back to predominately white Lincoln Park, Michigan.

After nearly 3 years of getting along better than any woman I've encountered, JoAn approached me with the idea of getting married and having a child. It was presented as an ultimatum.

I left her.

I loved her dearly, but I was 53 years old and didn't see how it was going to work out. So, I went back to dating and I applied for a doctorate program in Business Administration at California Pacific University.

Postgraduate classes didn't seem any harder than the ones from my

Master's degree, but I procrastinated on my dissertation for little while.

The dating scene was one disappointment and thrilling encounter after another thanks to Match.com. I found as I inched closer to women in my age group, I often had to have an exit plan. I didn't feel I was a good catch, but I knew how JoAn and I got along. The bar was high for civility and pheromones.

About a year and a half later, I ran into Katy, an old friend of JoAn's. I was eager to hear if she had moved on and found a potential husband to start a family. Katy had always been the kind of friend that thought we were destined for each other.

Katy couldn't believe that I let my age paralyze me into leaving her. It was as if she knew that I couldn't get JoAn out of my mind.

"She just finished running a

marathon in Honolulu, looking great, and she's not dating anybody. She's waiting for you to come to your senses Tom." Katy said with her usual directness.

I was shocked and quite frankly flattered that she thought that much of me.

"Tom, this is a once-in-a-lifetime opportunity, go have lunch with her and talk and you'll see and feel... She's special, you guys are special, just do it." Katy pleaded.

"I'll think about it, thanks Katie."

I gave her a hug and went on my way. After torturing myself for three days and nights about the 'what ifs', I called her.

JoAn and I met for lunch in Marina del Rey, which changed everything.

"I'll just say it, remember we weren't going to get together unless you were ready to get married and have a child." JoAn reminded me.

"Yes, I'm ready."

We excitedly planned a beach wedding and invited 70 of our closest friends and relatives.

We took tango lessons in the months before we got married.

Chris, Jeannie, and Justin were able to attend, which made it special for me. Chris brought his girlfriend, Melissa. She told me that Chris proposed to her at our wedding.

One of the major events of the wedding for me, was to tango with my new wife in the company of our best friends, family and my children.

After our wedding, we settled into an apartment in Encino. JoAn found work at Santa Monica College, and I became the Director of Distance Education at Northwest College in West Covina. I convinced the owner of the college that I could set up an online program for her, but she always balked at the price tag.

"You can't do something like this on a shoestring budget." I would explain.

Since there was no distance education program I worked with students with learning disabilities and tried to find technology related solutions for them.

During this time, I visited JoAn at Santa Monica College and met most of her friends in the Center for Students with Disabilities.

One day, I was approached by her friend and colleague, Ellen Cutler. Ellen knew that I was not enjoying my work as an administrator.

"Our part-timer is retiring soon, you should come work in our lab." Ellen said.

Ellen filled me in on the duties, schedule, and money involved. My mind was racing with the idea of a substantial change in my work life.

"I'll think that over, thanks." I replied with a smile.

At home, JoAn and I talked it over. Ellen's offer proposed that I work nine hours a day, two days a week for about $45,000 a year. When I added my $12,000 a year pension from the steel mill. I took the offer.

This decision, was one of the best that I ever made in my life. Through a long, difficult process, I was inevitably hired as a full-time tenure-track faculty member.

Ellen and I worked together for 11 years until she retired, and we remain close friends with monthly lunch dates.

JoAn and I struggled to have a baby. We were told by her gynecologist that our chances were slim without invitro fertilization. Time was ticking away for JoAn, we try not to worry about it. It was rough for both of us.

After JoAn met my three children, she was convinced that we would make a special child.

Pregnancy test strips were as common on our bathroom vanity as toothpaste. One day, JoAn came running out of the bathroom.

"It's positive honey, it's positive!" she announced.

After she tried two more strips to confirm, we jumped and cried with joy.

It was the spring of 2005 and we're going to have a baby. We knew that we had a high-risk pregnancy because of our age. JoAn put up with morning sickness throughout the whole pregnancy and took all of her doctors instructions with enthusiasm and grace. He found out that we were going to have a little girl.

In the first 3D ultrasound image, we were sure that she was going to look like Mick Jagger because of her large lips smiling at us from inside JoAn's womb. In the image she must have been pressed against the walls of the womb because she turned out to have smaller lips, and a magnificent smile.

Elisabeth Susan Peters was born in early 2006, named after both of her grandmothers. In the amazing years when Ellie was a baby, JoAn was an extremely happy mother. We made annual flights back to Michigan to visit the family. They all accepted JoAn with open arms and loved Ellie, especially my mother.

When Ellie was three, I had to take an extra trip in the spring back to Michigan because my mother had entered hospice care at home. My siblings helped to care for her and a nurse came once a week to check on her. I struggled through the final conversations that I had with my mother. Mom knew she was dying.

My mother passed away in late

April of 2009 and our family was grief stricken once again.

When Ellie was about four years old, JoAn had an unexpected heart attack one fateful morning. She lay on the halfway landing of the stairs as I called 911. I managed to stay as calm as I could since Ellie was with me.

Dr. Pelikan from St. John's Hospital inserted her first stent to save her life. Over the course of the next three or four years at several intervals, JoAn would have a total of thirteen stents inserted in arteries around her heart caused by tears and aggressive growth tissue causing a blockage within a stent. Another stent had to be put inside the blocked one. JoAn's heart issues led to her early retirement in 2016.

As Ellie approached kindergarten age, I received tenure. This financial boost meant we could move to a condo in Santa

Monica, only one mile from the college.

Since I had been active in the Steelworkers Union, I decided to do something similar with the faculty union at Santa Monica College.

I started playing golf with Union President Lantz Simpson. When Lantz termed out, Mitra Moassessi, was elected our union president. She wanted a new political director and Lantz suggested that I could do the job. I was called into Mitra's office and accepted the position and got involved in local and California state politics.

To enter Santa Monica politics from the union side, I had to get familiar with the city's longstanding political group called Santa Monicans for Renters Rights (SMRR). Once a month, the Steering Committee of SMRR meets and goes over an agenda that covers the city council, planning commission, rent control board, school district and Santa Monica College. I would attend and have to wait the more than four hours until Board of Trustees closely aligned with SMRR gave their reports. I would occasionally have to counter with the union's perspective. Following the advice of Nancy Greenstein, one of our college trustees, I volunteered to be of service on the SMRR Hotline.

The political director position brought out in me a talent I didn't even know I had, networking. I tried to cover almost every significant political event that had anything to do with local unions to help make our Faculty Association a relevant presence in the city. Mitra, our president and I walked picket lines for the California nurses Association, the hotel workers union called United HERE, and United Steelworkers triumph of organizing the first car washers union in the country.

The Democratic Club of Santa Monica welcomed me into their executive

committee as Vice President of
Membership. One of the club members,
Ben Allen would become a California State
Senator and later welcome myself and
fellow faculty leaders onto the Senate
floor in Sacramento. Fortunately, Senator
Allen sits on the higher education
committee and is a staunch ally.

The main part of my position was to
help hold Board of Trustees accountable
and find candidates to run against the
incumbents that frequently oppose our
positions. During one such election cycle,
we ran a retired History professor friend
of mine, Dennis Frisch and came close to
winning. Ousting an incumbent trustee is
almost impossible but am proud to say we
sent a message to the SMRR backed
candidates that we will run contested
elections if push comes to shove.

When Ellie turned about six years
old, JoAn and I decided to seek out a
church to attend to give her some

spiritual foundation and knowledge about the religions of the world. We joined the Unitarian Universalist Church of Santa Monica and what a wild ride that has been.

After having been led for 50 years by two consecutive humanist ministers, just before we joined, their search committee recommended, and the congregation approved Reverend Rebecca Bijur, a young woman and a graduate of Harvard Divinity. As new members we found ourselves in the middle of a battle, roughly between newer members that embraced Rev. Rebecca's leadership and older congregants that had real issues with her and wanted her out. I found myself volunteering for the Committee on Ministry, open to help out and possibly gain more knowledge about the conflict. However, it was that very committee that first did a survey and then some focus group type meetings that drew out more and more displeasure from a somewhat small but influential portion of the congregation. The details and complex history of the whole situation is a book in and of itself for someone else to write.

The church has given me some valuable insight. There have been moments, admittedly few and far in between, but magical, moving moments when either the choir or the whole congregation is singing and tears come to my eyes.

During one of the annual services set aside for our teenagers, a young woman stood up to the microphone and introduced the congregation to pansexuality. She described being pansexual as different than being bisexual. Pansexuals are open to relationships with anybody on the wide sexual spectrum. Of course, I found myself willing to accept the description given my past relationships with transsexual women. Go figure, pansexual.

On another occasion, during a service devoted to and run by young members of our congregation. A young member named Fred gave a passionate speech to help us all understand the mindset of teens today. Later in the service Fred was called back up to the mic and I had the overwhelming feeling that he was going to say, "I'm still Fred." When he did say exactly that I was somewhat surprised at first but then recalled that I heard Fred in other conversations and I knew his type of dry, deadpan humor. The church board president, Ron told me it was a right brain, right brain connection.

Reflecting, as one naturally does during the writing of a memoir, confirmed a trust I have in my intuition that has served me well.

CHAPTER 12

RETURN TO VIETNAM

My moment of clarity and peace.

It felt liberating to purchase a one-way ticket to Ho Chi Minh City.

In late January 2017, Forty-seven years since I left the country, JoAn gracefully encouraged me to go there and find what I was looking for.

In that city of over eight million people, I hoped to pass on a deeply personal message of support for the Vietnamese people and regret for my involvement in the war.

The vibrant, beautifully alive city, warmed my heart.

I've learned that forgiveness works its magic on the forgiver more than the forgiven. The forgiver does not necessarily condone or make peace with the forgiven. They move on and spend their energy on the present and future.

I purposely spent almost all of my time in Vietnam in District 1 of Ho Chi Minh City, probably the oldest part of the vast city of twenty four districts.

A taxi delivered me to a small boutique hotel next to the Ben Thanh Market. When I woke up the next morning, I went for a walk and met Quang, a gentleman about my age with a small motorbike. He offered to drive me around the city. After we negotiated a fair price, we were off on an unforgettable adventure, zipping around with five million other motorbikes in the city formerly known as Saigon.

Quang let me use his shoulders to stabilize myself on the back of the bike as we rode around the District. He pointed out the original U.S. Embassy and mentioned how vulnerable it was to attacks by the VC. Quang then took me by the well-fortified U.S. Embassy made familiar in the news coverage of the overthrow in 1975.

We stopped at the War Museum. Helicopters, tanks, a jet were parked outside of it. They referred to the war as, "The American War."

The museum was crowded with many international tourists and Vietnamese visitors. From the walks I had already taken, I had seen a few deformed Vietnamese men and women, who could have been poisoned by the Agent Orange that had been dumped on the country during the war. When I went up to the second floor and viewed many photos of bizarre and hideous deformed heads, limbs, and torsos, my heart ached. While at the museum, I felt like I was the only enemy soldier walking among these visitors.

It was impossible to sleep that night.

After I woke at noon, Quang called me from the lobby. He took me to the luxurious Hotel Majestic on the Saigon River. I would spend three carefree days in the classical French colonial designed hotel built in 1924.

I lounged by the pool until the evening. At dusk, I embarked on a quest to find the perfect martini. This would be my third or fourth attempt at such self-indulgence.

The martini bar at the Park Hyatt filled all my wildest dreams. I smiled when the bartender confirmed that they had

Hendrick's Scottish gin. After four amazing sips of a perfect martini, the couple next to me started chatting with me. An unforgettable conversation. The husband talked about the business adventure he had recently embarked on and his lovely wife explained why they chose Ho Chi Minh City for a vacation. When I mentioned I was in the city to finish my memoir, the conversation leaped into steady questions from the couple about my connection to Vietnam and the war. Three perfect martinis later, the couple invited me to London where they lived, we hugged and I bid them farewell.

I was ecstatic over the encounter and took the long walk back to my temporary home at the Hotel Majestic, in light, misty, magical rain.

When Quang asked me the next day if I had found what I was looking for in Saigon, I had to stop and think. When I was deployed, I had never step foot in the city itself.

"Let's drive out to Cu Chi." I smiled.

Cu Chi became famous for the tunnels dug by the Viet Cong and NVA during the war. After a long, jarring, scary ride we finally reached Cu Chi. When I saw the shiny tour buses I cringed. I bought my ticket and set out on the tour.

When the tour guide kept referring to the enemy, I had to stop and think again that I was probably the only one present that fit the description. I wandered into the woods and started to feel like I had been there before when I heard a series of shots fired. They had a rifle range where tourists could fire AK47s and M16s. This let me know it was time to find the entrance and return to Ho Chi Minh City.

Quang took a different route back, and I was thankful because we drove into the rubber plantations. Quang stopped at my request. He was nice enough to explain all the details of how rubber was made, which put me at ease, bless his heart. It reminded me of all those months that we patrolled the rubber plantations and never saw the enemy.

After I wandered the streets of Ho Chi Minh City a few more days, I took the bus to Vung Tau, the beach resort that I had enjoyed so many years before. Quang dropped me off at this odd bus station that was actually a small storefront. When we loaded into the van I thought this is going to be a miserable ride. Fortunately, the van took us to the outskirts of the city for a transfer to a huge, air-conditioned bus. Once I got to Vung Tau, I took a taxi to the Malibu Beach Hotel, where I had booked a three-day stay.

The Malibu Beach Hotel had great views, beautiful pool and a very pleasant staff.

My mind had glorified the beach area. The water was clear and blue in my memory, but it was brown and lifeless when I approached it forty seven years later. I swam and played in the surf, but it didn't spark any real memories. If anything, it made me realize that I dreamed up a beautiful place that wasn't beautiful.

What other memories had been tainted by time?

The three days went by fast. I had some interesting cuisine at various restaurants and the hotel next to mine made a pretty good martini. The next thing I knew, I was back in Ho Chi Minh City.

In an effort to be free from distractions back home my phone was turned off for the trip. The hotel Wi-Fi was used to make late night video calls to catch Ellie to talk briefly before school on

Pacific Standard Time. On some calls, Ellie had started school already so JoAn and I could talk alone.

"What's going on honey, you doing Okay?" JoAn asked.

"I think so, it's at least not the emotional roller coaster I feared. There's an exciting strangeness I'm tuned into." I replied.

"You going to stay longer?"

"I need another week and I'll be home to my girls." I said.

"Okay sweetheart, find what you're looking for and come home safe to us."

I will, love you baby, bye." I said and waited until JoAn ended the video call.

What was I looking for on this trip? Nothing seemed obvious up to this point, but I was spending a lot of time with the Vietnamese people. I wasn't sure if the experience added anything to the unfinished memoir, so I wanted to give it another week. JoAn's selfless support helped.

Nui Ba Den was a mountain east of Tay Ninh and served as a reference point for us on much of my tour. The Black Virgin Mountain, as it was also known, became a tourist attraction. It was easy to get a driver and interpreter to make the popular trip for about $185 or 4,154,730 dong.

Our travels in the Toyota was easier than riding on the back of Quang's bike, but it was only a little better. Thank goodness for seatbelts.

My interpreter, Sang, was well educated and had a calm spirit. The driver stayed behind as Sang and I set out on the modern tram that took us up the mountain. At the tram's end, sat beautiful temples. Sang excitedly told me of their origin and struggles during the war.

The view was stunning, but we were on the opposite side of the mountain of where French Fort was located. I learned a lot about the temples, but the memories I had of French Fort did not resurface.

Back at Ho Chi Minh City, I moved to the Palace Hotel down the street from the Majestic. For the next three or four days, I wandered the streets in all directions. I played a fun round of golf with a female caddie who never stopped smiling. Our conversations were limited by the language barriers, however, my poor putting made her giggle. Bless her heart, she skillfully lined up every putt for me, but I missed most of them.

One evening, I took in a wonderful experience at an old opera house that was only a few blocks away from my hotel. A tour guide gave us some fascinating history of the opera house. The group that performed was a sort of

Cirque du Soleil type performance that was very emotional and energetic. The cast members were very approachable after the performance.

Next door, was the famous Hotel Continental where I enjoyed a martini on the street level outdoor dining area.

Quang and I got together one more time.

"I want to ride out of the city once more Quang. Maybe the rubber plantations and Tay Ninh?"

"Of course, no problem." Quang replied.

So we headed back out of the dense city. Although my intention was to get all the way to Tay Ninh, my rear ached and it was hot and muggy. I asked him to pull over in a small hamlet. I thought that it might be our last conversation so I decided to probe a little deeper into his life.

"Does the government pay for retirement here?" I asked.

"You can retire at 80 years old and get about 300,000 dong," he said.

"That's about $15, yes?" I ask.

"Yes, but family takes care of you." Quang replied.

"How is your family and where do you live?" I inquired.

"Live very far," as he waves his arm toward the north.

"My wife is very good cook and our son is doing good in marketing, he lives in Danang." Quang said.

"We don't see him too much." He added.

I get a little philosophical with him.

"How has your life been?"

I spread my arms and open my palms wide, to indicate I meant overall.

"Life is good, yes, life is good most times." He said with a smile.

I had hoped he'd reflect a little on the war years. But, he didn't.

A destination has its moments, I seemed to find my moment of clarity and peace after my last conversation with Quang, where life and the noise in my mind, quieted down.

Tom – Ho Chi Minh City Zoo 2017

ABOUT THE AUTHOR

Tom was born in Detroit, MI in 1949, oldest of 10 children, son of a steelworker and homemaker/H & R Block manager, Milton and Susan Peters.

After high school graduation, Tom was hired at the same steel mill his father worked in and was drafted into the U.S. Army in late 1968 after marrying his first wife, Patricia.

During the 30 years Tom worked at National Steel as a crane operator, electrician and union activist, he earned a Bachelor's degree from Wayne State University and a Master's degree from Central Michigan University doing evening and weekend classes while raising three children, Christopher Jeannie and Justin.

Patricia and Tom divorced in 1984.

In 2004, he married JoAn Joseph at a beach restaurant in Malibu and they had a daughter, Elisabeth in 2006.

After teaching and working as an administrator at several schools around Los Angeles, Tom received a doctorate degree in 2008 while working at Santa Monica College where he's presently a tenured professor at the High Tech Training Center.

"Step Away from the War" is Tom's first book.

Made in the USA
Columbia, SC
20 February 2023

12740617R00102